vegetarian

other idg cookbooks by paulette mitchell:

The 15-Minute Gourmet: Noodles

The 15-Minute Gourmet: Chicken

The 15-Minute Single Gourmet

The Complete Book of Dressings

The Complete Soy Cookbook

vegetarian

paulette mitchell

IDG BOOKS WORLDWIDE

AN INTERNATIONAL DATA GROUP COMPANY

Foster City, CA • Chicago, IL • Indianapolis, IN • New York, NY • Southlake, TX

IDG BOOKS WORLDWIDE, INC.
An International Data Group Company
919 E. Hillsdale Boulevard
Suite 400
Foster City, CA 94404

The IDG Books Worldwide logo is a registered trademark under the exclusive license to IDG Books Worldwide, Inc., from International Data Group, Inc.

For general information on IDG Books Worldwide's books in the U.S., please call our Consumer Customer Service department at 800-762-2974. For reseller information including discounts and premium sales, please call our Reseller Customer Service department at 800-434-3422.

Library of Congress Cataloging-in-Publication Data

Mitchell, Paulette.
        15-minute gourmet : vegetarian / Paulette Mitchell.
            p.   cm. — (15-minute gourmet)
        New ed. of: The 15 minute vegetarian gourmet / Paulette
        Mitchell.   1987.
        Includes index.
        ISBN: 0-02-863529-9 (alk. paper)
        1. Vegetarian cookery. 2. Quick and easy cookery.   I.
Mitchell, Paulette.   15 minute vegetarian gourmet.   II. Title.
III. Series.
    TX837.M637   1999
    641.5'636—dc21   99-39008
                                                               CIP

Manufactured in the United States of America
10 9 8 7 6 5 4 3 2 1

Interior and cover design by Scott Meola
Cover photo by Nora Scarlett
Clock image © 1995 Chris Collins/The Stock Market
Silverware image © 1999 Photodisc
Cover photo: Asparagus-Cashew Stir-Fry (page 134)

To my son, Brett, who at age three when this book was first published,
tested my recipes as well as my patience.

contents

acknowledgments

Thank you to my friends, cooking students, and readers who, over the years, have inspired my cookbooks and savored my recipes. I am also grateful to Jane Dystel, my agent, and Linda Ingroia, my editor at IDG, who worked with me on the relaunch of this vegetarian classic. Thank you, also, to production editor Francesca Drago, designer Scott Meola, photographer Nora Scarlett, and food stylist Delores Custer and her assistants Lisa Homa and Judi Orlick.

introduction

WELCOME TO THE *15-MINUTE GOURMET: VEGETARIAN.*

Many friends and readers of the original book are trading in their much-used, dog-eared, well-spattered copies for this completely updated edition. Others who have been cooking quick meals from my books are now sending their sons and daughters off to their own kitchens with this and others in the series: *15-Minute Gourmet: Noodles, 15-Minute Gourmet: Chicken,* and *The 15-Minute Single Gourmet.*

No doubt, you've come to this book interested in cooking from scratch, using fresh ingredients to create good food, fast. The recipes here were inspired by my own need to balance demands on my time—writing, teaching, parenting, traveling, and staying connected to friends—and to keep my work in the kitchen efficient. Fifteen-minute recipes enable me to cook outstanding meals every night of the week, and I use many of these recipes to entertain with casual elegance. I hope these recipes will free you, too, from long hours in the kitchen and add nutrition and style to the vegetarian dishes you prepare.

Much has evolved since this book was first published in 1987. More readers are now interested in vegetarian cooking, in meatless ethnic cuisine, and in including whole foods in their diets. Even the most devout carnivores I know appreciate a warming vegetable curry or a hearty omelet stuffed with ricotta cheese and tomatoes.

My cooking class students often ask me for advice in dealing with the challenge of cooking for friends and family with clashing dietary needs and preferences—the finicky youngsters; the always-hungry teenager; the carbo-loading runner; the vegan visitor; and others concerned with calories, sodium, sugar, or gluten. Happily, with these recipes I can prepare a meal where everyone leaves the table nourished and content. Sometimes this may mean having a vegetarian recipe do double duty at the same table, as an entrée for the vegetarians and as a meat accompaniment for other guests.

These quick and easy recipes are meant to free your creativity (not limit your choices) and minimize the effort of making classic vegetarian cuisine. Focused on unprocessed, fresh foods, the recipes call for ingredients you'll find in your local supermarket. Many of these dishes were inspired by the profusion of ethnic influences (Italian, Indian, Chinese, Mexican, Thai). Some are speedy adaptations of complicated traditional dishes. You'll be using fresh ingredients and cooking them lightly to retain flavor, texture, color, and nutrients. The results will be decidedly "gourmet."

I've included strategies for the 15-minute approach to help you organize the simple steps and juggle several tasks simultaneously. Once you've become comfortable with the recipe procedures, your kitchen choreography will come naturally, speeding things along.

You'll also find that as you shop for the individual recipes, you'll be stocking your pantry with staples. Soon, you'll have the basics on your shelves and you'll need only to shop for fresh ingredients (a true time saver). I've found this approach is far more satisfying and takes only a few more minutes than messing around with prepackaged dinners or reheating several take-out components.

Vegetarianism and Its Many Styles

The term "vegetarian" identifies those who do not eat meat, but it is further defined by different approaches:

- Vegans, or strict vegetarians, consume only plant-based foods. They do not eat any animal meat nor animal-derived foods such as butter, cheese, eggs, milk. Some exclude honey, some yeast.

- Lacto vegetarians don't eat eggs, but do eat dairy products.

- Ovo vegetarians don't eat dairy products, but do eat eggs.

- Lacto-ovo vegetarians include animal-related foods such as eggs and dairy products in their diets. This is the most common of the vegetarian diets.

Many recipes here suit all vegetarians or are easily modified (within reason; it's impossible to make an omelet without eggs). Vegetable oil or margarine may be substituted for butter and soy- or rice-based products substituted for dairy.

The term "part-time vegetarian" applies to many of us who most often adhere to a vegetarian diet but occasionally consume some type of meat product. If you fall into this category, you will enjoy all of the recipes in this book and may sometimes want to use them as an accompaniment to red meat, chicken, or seafood.

Principles for Healthful Vegetarian Eating

There is really nothing complicated or mysterious about vegetarian cuisine. By following the three principles of balance, variety, and moderation, and adapting them to your lifestyle, you'll be well on the road to a healthier way of eating.

BALANCE

Ideally, each meal of the day should contain some of all the essential nutrients—protein, carbohydrates, and fats.

Protein

There are twenty-three different amino acids that compose protein—fifteen can be produced by the body—eight must be derived from the foods we eat. Only these eight are called "essential"; all fruits and vegetables contain most of the eight. In the newest edition of *Diet for a Small Planet,* author Frances Moore Lappé states, "If people are getting enough calories, they are virtually certain of getting enough protein." The key is eating a healthful, varied diet. In fact, plant protein foods contribute approximately 65 percent of the per capita supply of protein on a worldwide basis. Tofu, soybeans, and eggs are complete proteins on their own. Grains, beans, and seeds (incomplete proteins), when eaten in the same day, work to provide you with complete protein. Here are some examples of recipes in this book that combine meatless foods to make complete protein entrées:

Combining Grains and Milk Products

- Triple Cheese-Poppyseed Noodles (page 128)
- Couscous with Egg Sauce and Garden Vegetables (page 148)

Combining Grains and Legumes

- Pasta and Bean Soup (page 52)
- Chickpea-Zucchini Curry on pasta or rice (page 122)

Combining Seeds and Legumes

- Hummus (page 31)
- Moroccan Chickpea Soup (page 54)

Eggs, milk, and tofu, complete proteins on their own, are further enhanced in these recipes:

- Noodle Omelet with Ricotta Filling (page 152)
- Asian Rice and Vegetable Skillet (page 143)

Carbohydrates

Carbohydrates can be simple or complex and are the body's source of energy. Simple carbohydrates, such as sucrose, fructose, corn syrup, molasses, or lactose, offer quick energy but few nutrients. Fruit, however, is a source of vitamins, minerals, and fiber. Complex carbohydrates, such as cereals, pastas, and rice, are low in calories, contain some protein, and are rich sources of vitamins, minerals, and fiber.

Fats

Fats are a necessary part of our cell structure, carry fat-soluble vitamins, and add flavor to foods. They should, however, be used in moderation. Fats are divided into four groups as follows:

1. *Saturated fats* are found in both plant and animal foods: meat lard, butter, coconut oil, and palm oil, usually solid at room temperature. These have been shown to raise the levels of serum cholesterol and to increase the risk of heart disease and certain cancers. Use them in moderation, if at all.

2. *Polyunsaturated fats*, such as safflower oil, corn oil, soy oil, and sesame oil, are usually liquid at room temperature. The best choice, they are believed to reduce blood cholesterol.

3. *Monounsaturated fats*, such as olive oil, canola oil, and peanut oil, also are liquid at room temperature. According to some recent studies, they also may be able to reduce the amount of cholesterol in the blood.

4. *Trans fats*, considered by many researchers to be the worst for heart disease, are artificially processed polyunsaturates. They are created when oils are hydrogenated, which transforms them from their liquid state, at room temperature, into solids. These fats are found in margarine and in many packaged cookies and snacks; check the small print for the words "hydrogenated oils" or "partially hydrogenated oils."

Researchers have most recently found that replacing saturated fat with unsaturated fat and consuming less trans fat appeared to be more effective in lowering coronary risk than reducing totally dietary fat. This supports the idea that all fats aren't "bad" for you. Just be aware of what kinds of fats are in the foods you eat.

Many products are also now available in nonfat or low-fat forms. Women vegetarians concerned about increasing the amount of calcium in their diets to help

A WORD ABOUT OILS

- I recommend "cold-pressed" oils because heat processing destroys many of an oil's natural nutrients. Generally, cold-pressed oils are preservative-free and must be stored in the refrigerator after being opened. I use cold-pressed canola or safflower oil when I want a neutral oil that allows the other flavors in the recipe to shine through. Asian recipes that include soy sauce, sesame oil, and ginger call for a neutral cooking oil.

- In some recipes, the oil contributes flavor. Dark sesame oil, for example, is made from toasted sesame seeds and has an intense nutty flavor that seasons Asian salad dressings or enhances soups, sauces, or stir-fried foods when added at the end of cooking.

- My favorite oil is olive oil, and I call for it when its fruity flavor and distinctive aroma are compatible with the other recipe ingredients. Olive oils vary according to growing areas, grade, and quality; color tells little about it. "Extra-virgin" is the most flavorful and expensive of olive oils. It comes from the first pressings of top-quality olives and it has a full-bodied, fruity taste and low acidity. It is the best choice for use in uncooked recipes, such as salad dressings, pestos, and salsas, or it may be added for flavor in the final stages of cooking. The flavor of extra-virgin olive oil dissipates somewhat when heated.

- "Olive oil," or "pure olive oil," is a more refined, somewhat less flavorful oil; and it is usually used for cooking. "Light" olive oil is lighter in neither fat nor calories; the term refers to lighter in color and fragrance. In my mind it is a poor choice.

- Store olive oil in a cool, dark place and use within one year. Refrigerate it during hot weather; the oil will become thick and cloudy, but this does not affect the flavor or quality. Simply bring the oil to room temperature before using to restore the clarity.

offset osteoporosis (degenerative bone disease) will find some interesting uses for nonfat and low-fat dairy products. These also make tasty high-protein dishes.

VARIETY

Variety is the key to a healthful vegetarian diet. When grains, vegetables, and legumes take center stage, the plate is sure to be colorful and interesting. These whole foods are loaded with nutrients; vegetables and fruits are especially high in vitamins A, C, and E, proven natural allies against cancer and other diseases.

Unprocessed foods such as brown rice and whole wheat are high in fiber, important in preventing heart disease and colon cancer. The benefits of fiber are unaffected by cooking: raw or uncooked, it has the same value.

MODERATION

Processed foods loaded with salt, sugar, and fat can be obstacles in our struggle for good health. Working with whole foods makes it easier to take the middle road and not overdo, so that an occasional splurge is no big deal.

- *Salt:* The daily sodium requirement is about $^{1}/_{10}$ of a teaspoon; the average intake is 1 to 4 teaspoons daily! Excessive salt intake may lead to hypertension, which in turn is related to numerous potential health problems. The recipes in this book do not call for salt; some call for low-sodium soy sauce. I have not specified the use of reduced sodium or salt-free canned products; many products, including canned tomatoes, tomato sauce, and tomato paste, are available in these forms. Use them if you choose. If you are a heavy salter, you may be tempted to reach for the salt shaker with these recipes; just remember moderation. And if you do use salt, keep in mind that less sea salt is necessary because of its fuller flavor than ordinary table salt. Notice the natural saltiness in some vegetables and the delights of herbs and fresh flavors.

- *Sugar:* The average American consumes 120 pounds of processed sugar a year; that is one pound every three days, most of which comes from processed foods. Because processed sugar is usually found in low-nutrition, high-fat foods, it does not contribute anything to our diet except excess calories, and hence, excess body fat. Problems develop when highly sugared foods replace nutritious foods in the diet. Some experts even believe that sugar may affect blood cholesterol levels and also may be a factor in coronary heart disease. However, of the sweeteners, I prefer sugar to chemical-laden substitutes.

- *Fats:* Animal products are the major source of saturated fats; eliminating meat usually lowers the amount of saturated fat in your diet. If you eat dairy products, an important source of protein, use low-fat or nonfat products to cut down on cholesterol. I have not used cream or whole milk in the recipes and have provided suggestions for eliminating egg yolks whenever possible. I prefer the flavor and natural quality of butter and use it in moderation. (If you prefer, margarine can be substituted.)

- *Additives:* Several thousand chemical substances are added to our foods during manufacturing to preserve, flavor, and color them. There is conflicting evidence as to their effects, but many additives are thought to be potentially harmful. Begin to read labels and be aware of what is in the foods you buy. Be aware that the words "no preservatives" do not mean a food is additive-free; colorings and flavorings may still be added. Keep in mind that by using unprocessed, natural ingredients, you have more control over the content of your diet.

Put simply, the fresher the food, the more nutritious. Use natural unprocessed foods whenever possible. They taste better! If you cut down, it is not necessary to eliminate; the key word is moderation. Make wise choices. And remember, it is not what you *don't* eat, but what you *do* eat that counts.

Guides for Optimum Nutrition

To help you as you use this book, each recipe includes a nutrition analysis per serving, based on the stated number of servings that recipe yields. Recipes for basic condiments, sauces, and dressings, with yields expressed in cups rather than by servings, are analyzed per tablespoon, so that you can calculate the nutrients based on the serving size you choose. The ingredients have been analyzed in the form as listed, such as nonfat yogurt or skim milk. Dressings and sauces are included when they are part of a recipe. The figures will change with garnishes, suggested accompaniments, and variations. For example, using cholesterol-free egg substitute will reduce the cholesterol in recipes calling for whole eggs. Use the nutrition values to help you meet your dietary goals.

The Food Guide Pyramids

In 1995, the United States Department of Agriculture and the Department of Health and Human Services developed a guide to daily food choices called the Food Guide Pyramid. This guide for healthful eating is more helpful than the former program that distinguished the "Basic Four" food groups because the pyramid plan clarifies the relative importance of consuming foods in each category. The plan is easy for vegetarians to follow, especially the recommendation for consuming five or more servings of fruits and vegetables. The Bread, Cereal, Rice, and Pasta Group at the base of the pyramid provide the largest proportion of our diet. The Protein Group, which contains meat, poultry, and fish, also includes the vegetarian protein sources, including legumes, eggs, and nuts. Foods in the Fats, Oils, and Sugars Group should be consumed sparingly, which is easy to control when you make food from scratch, rather than relying on convenience foods.

The Vegetarian Diet Pyramid (page xxii), developed as a specific guide for vegetarians, recommends liberal consumption of whole grains, fruits and vegetables, and legumes. It advises eating meat alternatives—including legumes, nuts and seeds, egg whites, and soy milk or dairy products—daily. Vegetable fats and sweets should be consumed only occasionally or in small quantities.

FOOD GUIDE PYRAMID

A Guide to Daily Food Choices

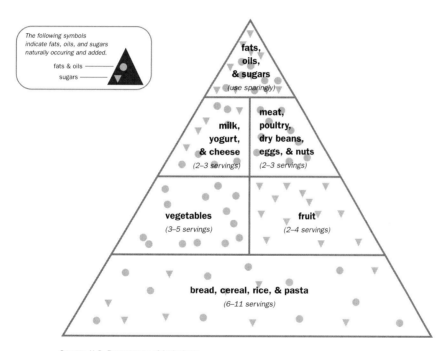

The following symbols indicate fats, oils, and sugars naturally occuring and added.

fats & oils

sugars

fats, oils, & sugars
(use sparingly)

milk, yogurt, & cheese
(2–3 servings)

meat, poultry, dry beans, eggs, & nuts
(2–3 servings)

vegetables
(3–5 servings)

fruit
(2–4 servings)

bread, cereal, rice, & pasta
(6–11 servings)

Source: U.S. Department of Agriculture

VEGETARIAN DIET PYRAMID

*Based on Traditional Eating Patterns of Healthy
Vegetarian Peoples of Many Cultures*

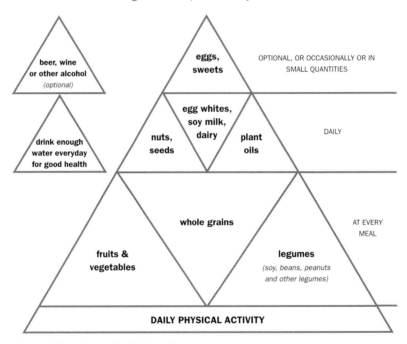

beer, wine
or other alcohol
(optional)

eggs,
sweets

OPTIONAL, OR OCCASIONALLY OR IN
SMALL QUANTITIES

drink enough
water everyday
for good health

egg whites,
soy milk,
dairy

nuts,
seeds

plant
oils

DAILY

whole grains

AT EVERY
MEAL

fruits &
vegetables

legumes
*(soy, beans, peanuts
and other legumes)*

DAILY PHYSICAL ACTIVITY

Source: Oldways Preservation & Exchange Trust

15-Minute Cooking and How It Works

Using the freshest ingredients in an organized way, you'll find you do not need a great deal of time to create colorful, tasty meals. These recipes rely more on the imaginative use of fresh ingredients than on elaborate techniques. The substantial main courses can stand alone, placing less emphasis on side dishes and the need to serve numerous courses. You won't spend a great deal of time cooking—but no one will ever know it. With some advance planning and minimum effort, dinner is a quarter hour away.

Advance planning is the key to successful 15-minute vegetarian gourmet cooking. Keep a running list of staples tacked inside a kitchen cabinet and replenish your supplies as you run out. Plan several menus for the week and make a list of the fresh ingredients you need to purchase. Try my suggestions for recipe variations or create your own using the odds and ends left from previous meals and favorite foods you might have on hand. Take both lists to the market. This way, you'll shop for the fresh foods you need and use them while they're at their peak. I've called for ingredients available in most supermarkets for simple one-stop shopping. These recipes are designed to swing with the seasons; don't hesitate to make substitutions based on fresh, seasonal local vegetables.

Stocking the 15-minute gourmet pantry is a gradual process as you'll find yourself accumulating the dried herbs and spices, sauces, and condiments that accent these recipes. Let your kitchen evolve as you become comfortable with this approach. Because frequently used ingredients such as pasta, rice, and tofu are bland on their own, it's critical that you use top-quality flavorings.

Fresh, Canned, Frozen, Packaged? These recipes call primarily for fresh foods, but some good-quality canned, frozen, or packaged ingredients can save time and make acceptable substitutes when produce is out of season or not up to snuff. It is much better to use good organic canned tomatoes than anemic hardballs in January. Frozen peas need no shelling. Canned beans and legumes make soaking and long-cooking times unnecessary (just drain and rinse before using).

Although expensive, many fresh herbs are available year round at supermarkets. When the weather is warm, farmers' markets sell reasonably priced bunches; or you can grow your own in your garden or in pots on the patio. Fresh herbs are called for in recipes where dried herbs are unacceptable. When dried herbs can be used, you'll find them in the recipe ingredient list; but feel free to use fresh instead. When substituting fresh for dried, use three times more of the fresh.

Pure vegetable stock now comes in cans. Vegetable stock concentrates come in jars and little tubs; and stock cubes and vegetable stock powder are available in bulk from a natural food store. I call for vegetable stock in many of these recipes; and on page 3, I offer the recipe for a simple basic stock that can be made ahead, refrigerated for a few days, or frozen. Because I usually don't take the time to make stock, I keep vegetable stock powder (with no preservatives and no salt) on hand; it keeps forever in my kitchen cabinet. Since it is unseasoned, the mild flavor blends with the herbs and other recipe ingredients. Look for the low-sodium or salt-free, nonfat stocks to allow other flavors to shine through.

When using commercially-prepared products, always read labels carefully. All of the ingredients are listed in order of quantity in the fine print. The Nutrition Facts label shows a breakdown of nutrients; the consistent label format required by the Food and Drug Administration (FDA) since 1994 will help you compare foods and make informed choices.

Read the Tips throughout the book for ingredient explanations. These may be helpful in knowing how to select, store, and use the ingredients in these recipes. Locate the Tips by referring to page references in the index.

The Organized Kitchen

The size of your kitchen does not matter; the way you make it work for you does. The more efficient your kitchen, the more capable and relaxed you are likely to feel. Arrange spices in alphabetical order. Store utensils close to where they are to be used, such as placing your knife block near the cutting board. Store frequently used items in accessible places so you can find—and grab—them quickly. Occasionally, this may mean having doubles of certain items, such as mixing bowls, work bowls for your food processor, and measuring spoons and cups.

Presentation

Think about presentation as you plan your meals. Garnishes—sprigs of fresh flat-leaf parsley, thinly sliced lemons, toasted pine nuts—add color and texture and enhance flavor. Quick and efficient needn't be slap dash, for example: a whole mint leaf alongside a vibrant curry dish, orange slices on a spicy salad, sprigs of basil set on pasta and tomatoes, or crunchy croutons on a creamy soup. With most of the recipes, you'll find suggestions for accompaniments—use one or a few. These artistic touches take but a few seconds. Your meals will look as though they were prepared by a trained gourmet chef rather than a hurried cook.

The Right Stuff

The right equipment speeds up cooking. Buy the best you can. To begin, you really need only one or two good pans (a 12-inch sauté pan or skillet for sautéing and a Dutch oven or stock pot for cooking pasta and making soups). Select pans with nonstick surfaces—you'll need less cooking oil and cleaning them will be a breeze. I've suggested the use of nonstick pans for many of the recipes. Commercial-quality pots and pans are the best. The initial investment price is high, but they will last a lifetime. Good knives are a must. Costly, yes, but you won't be replacing them every few years. Treat your equipment with care; this means sharpening knives frequently and hand-washing knives and most pans. Any professional chef worth his or her salt will tell you, fine cookware and equipment has an extraordinary feel and enhances your pleasure in the kitchen.

15 Tips for Flawless 15-Minute Cooking

1. Think ahead, plan ahead. After selecting your recipe, check your staples and make shopping lists for the ingredients you need. Check the ingredient information in the Tips that appear with the recipes; they will guide you in the selection and storage of your ingredients.

2. Variations are included with many of the recipes; consider them a springboard for your own imagination. Seasonal vegetables and family favorites can provide inspiration, and so can leftover ingredients from previous meals. Remember that some variations may require more preparation time, others less.

3. Prepare some ingredients to have on hand for future meals. If you are chopping onions for a stir-fry tonight, for example, chop extra for tomorrow's pasta dish. Prepare extra if you are grating cheese or toasting nuts and seeds; store them in tightly covered containers in the refrigerator.

4. Advance preparation of some of the basics—pesto, ginger sauce, marinara sauce, for example—saves time in the long run. Keep a supply on hand, ready to prepare a dish at a moment's notice.

5. Read the recipe before you begin, and think through the steps that may be handled simultaneously. Get things going—start water boiling, preheat the oven. Set out all of the ingredients; clean and start chopping foods before you begin to cook.

6. If possible, most ingredients should be at room temperature before you begin cooking them. Some, for recipes that will be served chilled, can be kept in the refrigerator until they are needed.

7. Chop vegetables for a recipe in similar sizes so that they will cook at the same rate.

8. Follow the sequence of steps as described. It's not always necessary to complete one step before going on to another; you may be able to chop and mix some of the ingredients while the others are cooking.

9. Preheat the oil before adding the ingredients for sautés and stir-fries. The food will cook more evenly and brown more quickly.

10. Bring water to a boil quickly by covering the pot with a lid.

11. When entertaining, organize and chop the ingredients and set out your equipment in advance. Some dishes can be prepared and held; others may be completed in phases, then assembled just before serving; check the Advance Preparation tips that accompany the recipes. These tips also tell you how long completed dishes can be stored, keeping food safety and good flavor in mind.

12. Cooking times are always approximate and may vary according to pan type, gas or electric heat, and differences among ingredients. Learn to judge by appearance, aroma, and taste. The recipes in this book provide you with cues.

13. Sample the completed dish and adjust the seasonings (especially the spicy ones) before serving.

14. The recipes multiply easily, though you may not need to increase herbs and seasonings in the same proportion as other ingredients. For example, if doubling a recipe, add $1^1/_2$ times the amount of herbs, taste and adjust. Note that multiplying a recipe may increase the preparation and cooking times.

15. The kind of cooking in this book tastes best eaten right away (exceptions are some of the sauces, soups, and dressings). Fresh flavors and crisp-tender textures nearly always deteriorate after being frozen and thawed. Don't plan for leftovers by increasing quantities. The steps are so quick, its easier to create new than revive old.

10 Techniques for the 15-Minute Vegetarian Cook

PROCESSING

A food processor is essential, making short work of certain kitchen tasks, such as chopping nuts or onions, grating cheese, or shredding vegetables. Look at each recipe with the food processor in mind. Chop dry foods first, then wet foods. Cleanup is easier if you do not have to wash the work bowl after each use; and, often, washing is unnecessary if the foods are to be combined in the recipe.

BLENDING

Designed for liquids, a blender is the most efficient way to emulsify salad dressings and purée soups and sauces. While you can use a food processor, you'll get a more refined purée from a blender. (If you're working with a large quantity, you may need to blend in batches.)

CHOPPING

Use a good sharp chef's knife, it's faster and safer. Time permitting, I chop and slice vegetables by hand, especially for stir-fries, because this is more precise. Chop on a good cutting board with the broad end of the knife blade, near the handle. Use short, up and down motions, working in a circle, to traverse all of the food as you slice, chop, or mince. Learn to cut large quantities at once, never just one stalk of celery or carrot if you need more. Dice by cutting in checkerboard fashion so that each swipe of the knife cuts 8 or 10 cubes.

SAUTÉING

This speedy method of cooking uses a low-sided pan atop the stove. It relies on very little fat—just enough for flavor and texture. True "spa cuisine" uses vegetable stock, eliminating oil entirely. If your goal is to reduce fats to that degree, try this method in any of the sautéed recipes.

Sautéing is terrific for preparing soups and skillet dishes. Sautéing the vegetables before adding the other ingredients eliminates the need for lengthy simmering and also adds flavor. Be sure to preheat the oil before adding the food. The food must be dry before it is added to the hot oil to eliminate splattering. Shake the pan over medium-high heat or stir the ingredients occasionally as they cook.

STIR-FRYING

Stir-frying is similar to sautéing. A high-sided wok is commonly used, but a 12-inch skillet does nicely. Here the food is flipped and stirred constantly and briskly as it cooks quickly over medium-high to high heat.

BROILING

The food cooks and browns in an oven broiler, directly under the heat source. To begin, adjust the broiler rack to the desired position and preheat the broiler. Watch closely because broiled foods burn easily.

GRILLING

Grilled vegetables have a special flavor not attainable by other cooking methods. You can grill them on an outdoor barbecue grill, but, for convenience, I usually use a stovetop grill pan. These pans are made from a variety of materials (some are non-stick, which I recommend) and are available in a range of shapes and sizes. What they have in common is raised ridges on the cooking surface that give foods cooked on the pan visually appealing grill lines along with a smoky, grilled flavor achieved quickly with little or no added fat. To use either an outdoor grill or a stovetop grill pan for cooking vegetables, slice the vegetables and brush lightly with oil. Cook, oiled sides down; then brush the other side and turn. Cook until the vegetables are tender and lightly browned.

SCRAMBLING

Used primarily for egg mixtures, scrambling means cooking gently in fat, lifting portions of food as they cook to allow uncooked portions to flow beneath.

STEAMING

Steaming cooks food in a porous receptacle over a small amount of boiling water. No added fat is necessary. Steaming retains the crisp-tender texture of vegetables. Stainless steel or bamboo steamers allow the steam to circulate around and through the food. Be sure to use a tight-fitting lid to prevent steam (and nutrients) from escaping.

MICROWAVING

Many conventional procedures in this book can be accomplished in a microwave. Vegetables, for example, can be microwaved instead of steamed on the stovetop with equal efficiency and good results. Always use a microwave-proof dish, add a small amount of water (about $^1/_4$ cup for a $1^1/_2$-quart container), and cover the dish tightly with microwave-safe wrap or a lid. Keep in mind that the vegetables continue to cook for a minute or two after they are removed from the microwave, so take care not to overcook them and drain them as soon as possible.

chapter 1

The Basics

KNOWING HOW TO PREPARE STAPLES SUCH AS RICE,

quick-cooking grains, pasta, legumes, and omelets will

save time when you're hurrying to get a meal together.

I've also shown how basic vegetable stock can be pre-

pared ahead of time and refrigerated or frozen.

Vegetable Stock

In many recipes, the key to rich flavor is good stock. If you don't have time to make your own, health food stores sell a variety of healthful stock cubes and granules. See page xxiv in the book introduction for a description. Admittedly, I usually use vegetable stock powder rather than making the stock from scratch.

If you have the time (15 minutes to prepare plus 1 hour to simmer), try the following recipe. It can be varied to use whatever vegetables you have on hand. Remember, the key to good stock is to achieve a balance of flavors without any single one predominating. Asparagus, broccoli, cabbage, and cauliflower create very strong flavors and should be used sparingly, if at all. The same holds true for starchy vegetables such as corn, peas, or potatoes: they can cloud the broth. Parsnips and carrots will create a sweeter stock.

Vegetables to be used in stock should not be peeled, but they should be trimmed of any bruises. Cut vegetables into large chunks; small pieces may disintegrate and make the broth cloudy.

To vary the flavor of the stock, herbs can be added. I recommend seasoning the stock sparingly, because herbs are usually added to recipes calling for vegetable stock. For a less intense flavor, add vegetables to the water in the pot without sautéing. For a more intense flavor, return the strained stock to the pot and simmer, uncovered, over low heat for an additional 30 minutes to 1 hour.

vegetable stock

Makes 2 quarts

2 tablespoons canola or safflower oil

1 large onion, sliced

1 potato, cubed

1 tomato, cubed

1 carrot, sliced (include greens,
   if available)

1 rib celery, sliced (include greens,
   if available)

1 turnip, sliced (peel if waxed)

2 cloves garlic, halved

2 quarts plus 1 cup water

1 bay leaf

1 large sprig flat-leaf parsley

1/2 teaspoon pepper

1. Heat the oil in a stock pot over medium-high heat. Add the onion, potato, tomato, carrot, celery, turnip, and garlic. Cook, stirring occasionally, for about 10 minutes or until the vegetables are tender. Stir in the remaining ingredients.

2. Cover and bring to a boil, then reduce the heat to medium and simmer for 1 hour.

3. Strain the stock and discard the vegetables, bay leaf, and parsley.

PER CUP: Cal 66/Prot .9g/Carb 7.8g/Fat 3.5g/Chol 0mg/Sod 25mg

ADVANCE PREPARATION   Vegetable Stock can be used immediately, refrigerated for up to 4 days, or frozen for up to 1 month. Stock is easily made ahead because it freezes well. For small quantities, freeze the stock in ice cube trays, then remove the cubes and use them as needed.

Grains

RICE

Like pasta, rice is low in calories and is enormously versatile. Furthermore, when combined with legumes, seeds, or dairy products, it forms a complete protein.

Rices are labeled according to size: long-grain, medium-grain, and short-grain. Each size has different properties and uses. Long-grain rice, which cooks up fluffy and dry, is preferable for recipes in this book; although medium-grain rice can also be used. Short-grain rice, such as arborio rice, cooks up stickier when cooked.

I recommend using long-grain brown rice because it contains three times the dietary fiber of white rice and more vitamins, minerals, and protein.

White rice has a shorter cooking time than brown rice, and some people prefer its flavor and texture. You'll find many varieties in the supermarket, including some enriched with vitamins. Parboiled rice, also called converted rice, has been soaked and steamed under pressure for the purpose of retaining nutrients; it takes longer to cook than regular white rice.

Originally developed in the foothills of the Himalayas in northern India, basmati rice is a specialty aromatic white rice that is gaining in popularity. It is an excellent alternative for the 15-minute cook because it can be prepared in just that amount of time.

Wild rice is not really a rice but the seed of a marsh grass that is native to America. It is harvested in areas around the Northern Great Lakes where it grows wild, and there is some commercial production as well. Rather than being bland like other rices, wild rice has a distinctive flavor; for that reason, after cooking I often mix it with cooked white or brown rice.

Do not use *instant* brown, white, or wild rice; these products are not only inferior in flavor and texture, but also much lower in nutrition.

HOW TO COOK RICE

Use the appropriate amount of water or vegetable stock—2^1/$_2$ times the amount of brown rice, 2 times the amount of white rice, and 3 times the amount of wild rice—and bring the liquid to a boil in a heavy nonstick saucepan over medium-high heat. It is not necessary to add salt or butter to the cooking liquid. Tightly cover the pan and reduce the heat to low. Simmer gently until all the water is absorbed: 45 minutes for long-grain brown rice, 20 minutes for long-grain white rice, and 40 minutes for wild rice. Use these times as a guideline; the weight and size of the pan are variables. *Never stir rice while it is cooking!* This will result in a sticky and gummy product. Removing the lid during cooking will also lower the quality of the rice.

When the rice is cooked, remove the pan from the heat and allow the rice to stand, covered, for about 10 minutes. Before serving or using it in a recipe, fluff the rice with a fork. One cup of uncooked rice (long-grain brown, long-grain white, or wild rice) yields about 3 cups of cooked rice.

If you use rice regularly you might want to invest in an electric rice cooker. It will cook the rice perfectly without supervision. Some rice cookers have a "warm" setting for holding the cooked rice at just the right temperature until it is needed.

Rice can be cooked ahead of time. I always make more than I need for a meal because cooked rice will keep for up to one week in the refrigerator or up to two months in the freezer in bags or freezer containers. Thawed rice does not stand well on its own, but it is acceptable in soups and well-seasoned skillet dishes.

The microwave effectively reheats cooked rice. Make sure the microwave-proof container is covered so that the steam will keep the rice moist and microwave for about 1 minute per cup of rice. On the stovetop, reheat rice in the top of a double boiler. Or put the cooked rice in a heavy nonstick saucepan and sprinkle with 2 tablespoons water per cup of cooked rice; cover tightly and heat, stirring occasionally, for 5 to 10 minutes.

If you are in a hurry and don't have any precooked rice on hand, several grains other than rice are quick-to-prepare alternatives. Try couscous, bulgur wheat, or quinoa.

COUSCOUS

Couscous, sometimes called Moroccan pasta, is a tiny, bead-like pasta made from semolina flour. It is available made from both white and whole wheat flours. You'll find it in the supermarket, usually near the rice. To prepare couscous, combine equal quantities of couscous and hot (nearly boiling) liquid. (You can use water or vegetable stock; tomato juice will add a tomato flavor.) Let stand, covered, for about 5 to 10 minutes or until the liquid is completely absorbed and the couscous is tender. The couscous will double in volume as it absorbs the liquid. Fluff with a fork before using.

BULGUR (CRACKED) WHEAT

Bulgur is a form of processed wheat. It has a chewy texture and nutty flavor and is created by boiling wheat kernels, drying them, removing some of the bran layers, and finally cracking the kernels. Since it is precooked in processing, bulgur wheat can be hydrated by soaking the grain in liquid for a few hours. Or it can be cooked on the stovetop: bring the liquid and grain to a boil over high heat, then reduce the heat and simmer for about 15 to 20 minutes. With either method, use 2 parts liquid (water or vegetable stock) to 1 part bulgur wheat.

QUINOA

Quinoa (keen-wah) is an ancient Peruvian grain that is known for containing more protein than any other grain. Look for it in natural food stores and in some supermarkets. To cook quinoa, use water to quinoa in a 2 to 1 proportion (the quinoa will expand to about 4 times its volume when cooked); combine in a pan and bring the liquid to a boil over high heat. Reduce the heat to low, cover, and simmer for about 5 minutes or until the water is absorbed. When cooked, the grains will be translucent and the outer rings will separate. The flavor is bland but slightly sweet, and the texture is light and fluffy.

Pasta

No longer thought of as strictly Italian, pasta has very nearly replaced potatoes in the American diet. It is not high in calories: a 2-ounce serving has only 200 calories. And when combined with light, meatless sauces featuring fresh vegetables, it is a wonderful choice for the health-conscious cook.

In its basic form, pasta is a mixture of durum wheat flour (semolina) and water. It is kneaded, shaped, and then dried or boiled fresh. Eggs are sometimes added to produce more delicate noodles. Spinach and tomatoes, and sometimes carrots or beets, are added for color.

Many supermarkets sell both fresh pasta and enriched dried pasta in a wide variety of shapes. Remember, fresh pasta keeps for only about three days in the refrigerator; it can be frozen for longer storage.

HOW TO COOK PASTA

For a main dish, allow 2 to 3 ounces dry pasta per serving or 3 to 4 ounces fresh pasta. Pasta "sizers" are nifty gadgets that will help you determine the correct amount of pasta strands to drop in your pot. For short cuts of dried pasta, use these quantities for 4 servings:

egg noodles: 6 cups

bow tie pasta (farfalle): 4 cups

elbow macaroni: 2 cups

corkscrew pasta (rotini or rotelle): 3 cups

spaghetti: $1^{1}/4$-inch bunch

For cooking pasta, use a large pot that is deeper than it is wide. If you make pasta frequently, you might want to purchase a pasta pot with a built-in colander; these pots are available in most gourmet shops.

Use plenty of water for cooking pasta: 2 quarts for 8 ounces pasta is about right. Add the pasta to water that has come to a boil over high heat. It is not necessary to add salt or oil to the cooking water. If you like, you can add 1 to 2 teaspoons of salt per quart of water, after it comes to a boil. Reduce the heat to medium-high while the pasta is cooking. It's not necessary to cover the pot; in fact, it's easier to check the pasta if the pot is uncovered. Make certain that the water continues to boil throughout the cooking period. Stir the pasta occasionally to avoid clumps that will cook unevenly; avoid overstirring, because it will make the pasta gummy.

Cooking time depends on the type of pasta you have chosen. Fine strands cook very quickly; heavy, thick shapes require more time. Fresh pasta may be done in just 5 to 10 seconds. Imported dried pastas often take a little longer than American-made pastas. The average cooking time for dried pasta is about 8 to 12 minutes. Some Asian noodles require only soaking for a few minutes in boiling water.

Use package directions only as a guideline and rely on your own taste-testing to tell you when the pasta is done. If you pinch a pasta strand and see a white dot in the center, it is not cooked. Pasta is cooked perfectly when it is *al dente*, which means the strands are tender but still slightly chewy. Overcooking is the most common pasta failing; mushy pasta spoils the taste of almost any sauce, no matter how excellent.

When it is done, immediately drain the pasta well because wet noodles will water down your sauce. An advantage of using a pasta cooker is that it comes equipped with a stainless-steel liner that is pierced with holes. The pasta is easily removed from the pot and the liner acts as a colander, draining the noodles when done. There is no need to rinse pasta; however, if you plan to use it for a chilled salad, rinsing with cool water will help to speed up the process.

Many of my students ask if pasta can be cooked ahead of time. I feel that pasta is one of the few things you should really cook, drain, and sauce just before serving. But even though pasta is not a do-ahead item, it is still ideal for the 15-minute cook. All of the pasta toppings in this chapter can be made in 15 minutes or less while the pasta is cooking. Some of the toppings do not even need to be cooked! If you time it just right, you should have both the pasta and the

topping ready at the same time. Some of the pasta toppers can be made in advance, refrigerated, and reheated as the pasta cooks. Remember, though, that even before readying your ingredients you should fill your pasta pot with water and bring it to a boil.

I have made suggestions for the type of pasta to be used with each recipe, but an important thing to remember is that pasta shapes are interchangeable. Bear in mind that some shapes serve purposes: As a rule, shapes with ridges trap sauces; they are ideal for light sauces. Rich sauces should be served with flat pastas or shapes that trap less sauce.

Legumes

Although most legumes (or beans) are incomplete protein, they combine with many foods—milk, grains, seeds, or nuts—to form a complete protein. In addition to vegetable protein, legumes are good sources of carbohydrates, several B vitamins, and iron. Best of all, they are high in fiber and low in fat.

Because they are quick and nutritionally equal to freshly cooked beans, I have used canned beans for the recipes in this book. Since they have added salt, drain and rinse them with cold water before serving.

If you prefer using dried beans you'll need to plan ahead because most require presoaking and lengthy cooking. Dried beans keep for several months in a tightly closed container at room temperature. Once cooked, you can store them for up to 2 days in a covered container in the refrigerator. They may be cooked in large quantity when you have time and frozen for later use.

As a rule, 1 cup of dried beans yields about $2^1/_2$ cups cooked. To cook dried beans, rinse them to remove stones, dirt, and any discolored beans. Cover the beans with warm water (use about 3 cups of water for each cup of dried beans). Let them soak for at least 4 hours or overnight in the refrigerator. Or, to speed up soaking time, put the beans and water in a large saucepan, bring to a boil, and simmer for 2 to 3 minutes. Remove pan from the heat, cover tightly, and allow to stand for about 1 hour.

After draining the soaked beans, put them in a heavy-bottomed saucepan and cover with about 1 quart fresh water for every 2 cups of beans. (Don't add salt because it will delay the softening of the beans.) Bring the water to a boil over high heat, then lower the heat to medium and simmer for $1^1/_2$ to 3 hours, depending on the type of bean: for example, kidney beans require $1^1/_2$ to 2 hours; chickpeas and pinto beans 2 to 3 hours. Because lentils are soft-shelled and small, they require no soaking before cooking. Simply use 3 parts water to 1 part dry lentils and cook for about 30 to 60 minutes or until tender. In general, beans are done when they are soft enough to be crushed easily between the tongue and the roof of the mouth. Cut lengthwise, the inside should have an even color and consistency, with no white or hard portions.

A slow cooker can be used to cook legumes and has the advantage of requiring minimal attention. A pressure cooker can dramatically shorten cooking time.

Omelets

Omelets adapt themselves to breakfast, lunch, dinner, and even dessert. Leftovers of many of the recipes in this book make wonderful omelet fillings and, for variety, many sauces are ideal omelet toppings. An omelet can also be served without filling or sauce when your time is limited. To make an elegant omelet, simply add chopped fresh herbs to the egg mixture.

You do not need a special omelet pan. If you have eggs on hand and a well-seasoned or nonstick skillet, you are ready to begin.

HOW TO PREPARE A FRENCH OMELET

Begin with the eggs at room temperature. Use 2 eggs and 1 tablespoon of cold water per serving. For a creamy, tender omelet, lightly beat the eggs and water with a fork or whisk just long enough to combine.

Heat butter (or margarine, if you prefer) in the pan over medium-high heat (high heat makes a less tender omelet) until it bubbles. Swirl it to coat the pan, then immediately add the

eggs. They should start to set around the edges as soon as they are poured into the pan. Push the cooked edges toward the center without cutting through the omelet, tilting the pan so that uncooked portions can flow to the bottom and reach the hot pan surface. Cook about 3 minutes or until the eggs are still moist but no longer runny.

Per Serving: Cal 199/Prot 13.5g/Carb 2.7g/Fat 14.9g/Chol 429mg/Sod 342mg

A FLUFFY OMELET

Make this light creation by beating the egg whites and yolks separately, cooking in a skillet, and completing the procedure in the oven. See page 170.

AN OMELET FOR A CROWD

This is not as hard as it sounds. For efficiency, prepare one omelet in a large pan. Roll the large omelet and slice it into single servings. Or keep the omelet flat and top it with the filling and sauce, then cut it into wedge-shaped, open-faced servings.

Adding the Filling

Omelet fillings should be added to the pan on top of the egg mixture while it is still moist and creamy. If you are using a hot filling or topping, heat it separately before adding it to the omelet. Filling recipes and sauces are on pages 154–159. Other appropriate sauces appear on pages 19–22. See suggestions for combinations on page 153.

Making a folded omelet takes practice. Spread the filling along the center third of the omelet, perpendicular to the pan handle. Slip a spatula under the third nearest the handle, and fold it gently over the filling. Slide the omelet onto a serving plate by sliding the outermost third onto the plate, then lift the pan handle to roll the remainder over, so the omelet lands seam side down.

TIPS FOR USING EGGS

With proper care and handling, eggs pose no greater health risk than other perishable foods. Since salmonella bacteria are found in some eggs, it is wise to take the following precautions:

- Buy only clean, uncracked eggs that have been refrigerated.

- Do not leave eggs in any form at room temperature for more than two hours.

- Cook eggs until no visible liquid remains.

- Do not taste mixtures or batters containing raw egg.

Eggs will keep for up to one month in the refrigerator, but they lose their fresh flavor after one week. Store them with the large end up in the coldest part of your refrigerator, not in the molded door rack. Since eggs can absorb odors through their porous shells, storing them in the carton helps protect them from the aromas of other foods.

Cholesterol-free egg substitutes are made from real egg whites. The flavor is enhanced by the addition of a small amount of corn oil, and some yellow coloring is added to give the appearance of whole eggs. Reduced-cholesterol egg products are made from whole eggs from which nearly all of the cholesterol has been removed. These egg substitutes are found both in the freezer and in the refrigerated sections of most supermarkets.

mustard

Makes 2 cups

I like to keep this zesty mustard on hand because I find endless ways of using it. I often multiply the recipe to share jars with friends.

1 cup powdered mustard	3 eggs
1 cup white rice vinegar	1 cup sugar

chapter 1 *The Basics*

> **TIPS**
>
> - To sterilize a glass jar, wash and rinse it. Then immerse the jar in boiling water for at least 10 minutes, or until needed.
> - When using a double boiler, adjust the level of simmering water so it does not touch the bottom of the top pan.

1. Combine the mustard and vinegar in a small bowl; whisk to remove any lumps. Cover and let stand at room temperature overnight.

2. Sterilize a glass container with a tight-fitting lid (see Tips).

3. Pour the mustard-vinegar mixture into a blender; add the eggs and sugar. Blend until smooth.

4. Heat water until it simmers in the bottom pan of a double boiler over high heat (see Tips), then reduce the heat to medium. Pour the mixture into the top pan insert; stir constantly for about 5 minutes or until it thickens to pudding consistency.

5. Remove the top pan from the double boiler and allow the mustard to cool for about 5 minutes, stirring occasionally. Pour the mustard into the sterilized container; cover and refrigerate.

PER TABLESPOON: Cal 30/Prot .6g/Carb 6.1g/Fat .5g/Chol 19mg/Sod 6mg

ADVANCE PREPARATION   Pour the mustard into clean, sterilized containers, cover tightly, and refrigerate for up to 2 months.

Variation

- Substitute $3/4$ cup honey for the sugar.

13

mayonnaise

Makes 2 cups

When making mayonnaise, use pasteurized eggs or cholesterol-free egg substitute to avoid consuming raw eggs and to safeguard your health.

2 pasteurized eggs (at room temperature)

$1/2$ cup white rice vinegar or fresh lemon
   juice

1 tablespoon honey

$1/4$ teaspoon ground white pepper,
   or to taste

Dash of powdered mustard

$1^1/2$ cups canola or safflower oil
   (at room temperature)

Blend all of the ingredients, except the oil, in a blender until smooth. Continue blending and add the oil very slowly, in a steady, thin stream, until the mixture is smooth and thickened. (It will not be as thick as commercially-prepared mayonnaise.) Adjust the seasoning to taste.

PER TABLESPOON: Cal 105/Prot .4g/Carb 1g/Fat 11g/Chol 13mg/Sod 4mg

ADVANCE PREPARATION   This mayonnaise will keep for up to 3 weeks in a tightly covered jar in the refrigerator.

Variation

- For herb mayonnaise: Stir 3 tablespoons minced fresh basil, dill, tarragon, parsley, or watercress, or a combination, into the completed mayonnaise. Use as is or thin with white rice vinegar or more fresh lemon juice to use as a sauce that is delicious drizzled over steamed vegetables, especially asparagus.

mixed
fruit
chutney

Makes 2 cups

Chutney is an excellent accompaniment to curried entrees, and it is also an ingredient in several recipes in this book. Vary the recipe by substituting currants for raisins, peaches for the pears, or by stirring $1/4$ cup chopped walnuts, pecans, or slivered almonds into the cooked chutney.

8 dried apricot halves, chopped

$1/2$ apple, peeled and diced

$1/4$ cup dark raisins

1 tablespoon grated lemon rind

$1/4$ cup fresh lemon juice

3 tablespoons water

3 tablespoons cider vinegar or white rice vinegar

2 tablespoons light brown sugar

$1/2$ teaspoon ground cinnamon

Dash of pepper, or to taste

2 pears, cored, peeled, and diced

1. Combine all of the ingredients, except the pears, in a medium saucepan. Cover and cook over medium high heat, stirring occasionally, until the liquid comes to a boil.

2. Reduce the heat to medium and continue to cook, covered, stirring occasionally, for about 10 minutes.

3. Add the pears; cover and cook, stirring occasionally, for about 5 more minutes or until all of the fruits are tender. Adjust the seasoning to taste.

4. Serve warm or refrigerate.

PER TABLESPOON: Cal 21/Prot .1g/Carb 5.5g/Fat 0g/Chol 0mg/Sod 1mg

ADVANCE PREPARATION   This chutney will keep for up to 2 weeks in a tightly closed container in the refrigerator.

15

basil
pesto

Makes ¹/₂ cup

Basil pesto is traditionally a rich, aromatic mixture of fresh basil, pine nuts, garlic, olive oil, and Parmesan cheese put through a blender or ground with a mortar and pestle and served tossed with warm pasta. (Because I like to freeze pesto, I leave out the Parmesan, since the flavor deteriorates when frozen. If you plan to use the pesto fresh, add about ¹/₄ cup freshly grated Parmesan when puréeing the ingredients.) To use for a pasta salad, toss the pesto with warm pasta, then chill.

2 cups fresh basil leaves (fresh
   is essential); (see Tip)

¹/₄ cup pine nuts

2 cloves garlic

1 tablespoon extra-virgin olive oil

Process all of the ingredients in a food processor until the mixture is a coarse purée. Using a rubber scraper, push down the sides occasionally.

PER TABLESPOON: Cal 53/Prot .8g/Carb 1.7g/Fat 4.8g/Chol 0mg/Sod 4mg

ADVANCE PREPARATION   This pesto will keep for up to 1 week in a covered container in the refrigerator; pour a thin film of oil on top of the pesto to prevent discoloration. For longer storage, spoon the mixture into foil-lined custard cups or muffin tins; cover tightly with foil and freeze. Once frozen, remove the foil-wrapped packets and store in a freezer bag for up to 2 months. To use, thaw overnight in the refrigerator or quickly in the microwave. Bring the pesto to room temperature before tossing with hot, freshly cooked pasta.

Variations

- Add $^3/_4$ cup freshly grated Parmesan cheese.

- Substitute walnuts or hazelnuts for the pine nuts.

Uses

- For an appetizer: Stuff Basil Pesto into hollowed cherry tomatoes, centers of stemmed raw mushrooms, or into ribs of celery. Garnish with freshly grated Parmesan cheese and freshly ground pepper.

- For a dip to serve with raw vegetables: Stir $^1/_4$ cup of Basil Pesto into $^1/_2$ cup plain yogurt. Add freshly grated Parmesan cheese and freshly ground pepper to taste.

- Use Light Pesto Vinaigrette (page 94) as a salad dressing or as a marinade for steamed vegetables.

- To make pesto herb spread: In a food processor, combine 2 to 3 tablespoons Basil Pesto with $^1/_2$ cup softened unsalted butter (or margarine), 3 tablespoons freshly grated Parmesan cheese, and a dash of fresh lemon juice; process until smooth. Pour into a container, cover tightly, and chill. Serve as a spread for warm French bread to accompany soups, salads, and pasta dishes or toss with warm green beans, asparagus, potatoes, or spinach.

> **TIP**
>
> To store fresh herbs, wrap the stem ends with a moist paper towel and refrigerate in a sealed plastic bag. Or place the bunch, stems down, in a glass containing 1 inch of water; cover with a plastic bag, securing the bag to the glass with a rubber band. Change the water every 2 days. With proper storage, fresh herbs will last for about 1 week; but for the best flavor, use them within a few days. Just before using, wash fresh herbs in cool water, then dry them with paper toweling or in a salad spinner.

spinach-parsley
pesto

Makes ³/₄ cup

Use this recipe when you are in the mood for Basil Pesto, but fresh basil and pine nuts are unavailable. I like to toss the mixture with spaghetti; garnish it with halved cherry tomatoes and a generous sprinkling of freshly grated Parmesan cheese.

2 cups coarsely chopped stemmed fresh spinach leaves, loosely packed

1 cup fresh flat-leaf parsley leaves, loosely packed (see Tip)

¹/₂ cup freshly grated Parmesan cheese

¹/₄ cup coarsely chopped walnuts

2 cloves garlic

3 tablespoons minced fresh basil (or 2 teaspoons dried basil)

1 tablespoon extra-virgin olive oil

¹/₄ teaspoon pepper

TIP

Flat-leaf parsley has a more pungent flavor and is preferable to the more common curly-leaf parsley. Wash fresh parsley and shake off the excess moisture; then wrap in damp paper towels and store for up to 1 week in a plastic bag in the refrigerator. Avoid using dried parsley, which has little of the distinctive parsley flavor.

Process all of the ingredients in a food processor until the mixture is a coarse purée. Using a rubber scraper, push down the sides occasionally.

PER TABLESPOON: Cal 62/Prot 2.7g/Carb 1.8g/Fat 4.9g/Chol 3mg/Sod 84mg

ADVANCE PREPARATION   See Basil Pesto (page 16).

marinara sauce

Makes 2 cups

This meatless tomato sauce serves as an omelet, pasta, or vegetable sauce. It can also be used as an appetizer (served warm, at room temperature, or chilled), with slices of crusty French bread.

> **TIP**
>
> To make tomato sauce from tomato paste: Combine 1 (6-ounce) can of tomato paste with 2 cans of water.

1 tablespoon olive oil

1 carrot, finely shredded

1 rib celery, finely chopped

1/4 green bell pepper, finely chopped

1/4 cup finely chopped onion

1 teaspoon minced garlic

1 (6-ounce) can tomato paste

1 (8-ounce) can tomato sauce (see Tip)

1 teaspoon dried oregano

2 tablespoons coarsely chopped fresh flat-leaf parsley

1/2 teaspoon dried thyme

1/2 teaspoon dried basil

1/4 teaspoon pepper, or to taste

Dash of cayenne pepper or red pepper flakes, or to taste

1/2 cup water

1. Heat the oil in a medium nonstick saucepan over medium-high heat. Add the carrot, celery, bell pepper, onion, and garlic; cook, stirring occasionally, for about 5 minutes. Stir in the remaining ingredients.

2. Reduce the heat to medium; cover and simmer for about 5 more minutes or until the vegetables are tender. Adjust the seasonings to taste.

PER TABLESPOON: Cal 15/Prot .4g/Carb 2.2g/Fat .5g/Chol 0mg/Sod 50mg

ADVANCE PREPARATION   This sauce will keep for up to 3 days in a covered container in the refrigerator.

zesty **tomato** sauce

Makes 1¹/₄ cups

Try this flavorful sauce as a topping for pasta or omelets.

1 cup vegetable stock (see pages xxiv and 3) or water

1 (6-ounce) can tomato paste

¹/₂ teaspoon paprika

¹/₂ teaspoon red pepper flakes, or to taste

¹/₂ teaspoon pepper, or to taste

¹/₄ teaspoon ground coriander

¹/₄ teaspoon ground cumin

Combine all of the ingredients in a medium saucepan. Bring the mixture to a boil over medium-high heat; then reduce the heat to medium and simmer, stirring occasionally, for about 10 minutes. Adjust the seasonings to taste.

PER TABLESPOON: Cal 8/Prot .3g/Carb 1.7g/Fat 0g/Chol 0mg/Sod 8mg

ADVANCE PREPARATION   This sauce will keep for up to 3 days in a covered container in the refrigerator.

garlic-tomato
sauce

Makes 2 cups

Serve this versatile garlicky sauce on the Savory Nut Burgers (page 150) or tossed with pasta.
As a vegetable topper, it is a luscious complement to steamed green beans.

2 tablespoons butter

$1/4$ cup finely chopped onion

1 teaspoon minced garlic (see Tips)

1 tablespoon all-purpose flour

1 teaspoon paprika

1 ($14^1/2$-ounce) can diced tomatoes, drained, reserve juice

$1/4$ teaspoon pepper, or to taste

1. Melt the butter in a medium nonstick saucepan over medium-high heat. Add the onion and garlic; cook, stirring occasionally, until the onion is softened.

2. Reduce the heat to medium; add the flour and paprika. Cook, stirring constantly, for 1 minute. Stir in the reserved liquid from the tomatoes. Cook, stirring constantly, for about 2 minutes or until sauce is slightly thickened.

3. Add the tomatoes and pepper; stir until heated through. Adjust the seasoning to taste.

PER TABLESPOON: Cal 12/Prot .2g/Carb .9g/Fat .8g/Chol 2mg/Sod 28mg

ADVANCE PREPARATION   This sauce will keep for up to 3 days in a covered container in the refrigerator.

TIPS

- Marinated minced garlic in jars, sold in the produce department of most supermarkets, is an acceptable alternative to fresh garlic. One-half teaspoon of pre-minced garlic equals a fresh clove. Avoid using dried garlic, which is bitter and will not provide the distinctive garlic flavor and aroma.

- To peel a garlic clove easily, place the flat blade of a chef's knife on a garlic clove; pound with your fist to flatten the clove. This separates the skin and automatically crushes the garlic.

- To store garlic for up to 2 weeks, peel the cloves, place them in a small jar, cover with olive oil or safflower oil, and refrigerate.

tomato-yogurt
sauce

Makes 1¹/₂ cups

Because this sauce is made with ingredients I always have on hand, it heads my list as a quick pasta or omelet topper.

2 teaspoons canola or safflower oil

1 teaspoon minced garlic

1 (6-ounce) can tomato paste

1 teaspoon dried oregano

¹/₂ teaspoon pepper, or to taste

1 cup nonfat plain yogurt (see Tip)

GARNISH (OPTIONAL)   sprigs of fresh basil

> ### TIP
>
> Bring yogurt to room temperature before heating it and don't let it come to a boil; this will help prevent any separation or curdling.

1. Heat the oil in a small nonstick saucepan over medium-high heat. Add the garlic; cook, stirring constantly, for about 1 minute. Stir in the tomato paste, oregano, and pepper. Cook, stirring constantly, until the sauce is heated through.

2. Reduce the heat to low and add the yogurt. Stir constantly just until the sauce is warmed through. Adjust the seasoning to taste.

PER TABLESPOON: Cal 16/Prot .8g/Carb 2g/Fat .5g/Chol 0mg/Sod 8mg

ADVANCE PREPARATION   This sauce will keep for up to 2 days in a covered container in the refrigerator.

Variation

*   Substitute olive oil for the canola or safflower oil and basil for the oregano.

orange-tahini
sauce

Makes 1¹/₂ cups

This unusual sauce is delicious tossed with pasta or in stir-fries, but my favorite use for it is over steamed vegetables, such as green beans or broccoli.

1¹/₄ cups fresh orange juice

1 cup tahini (see Tip)

1 teaspoon minced garlic

Water, as needed

¹/₂ teaspoon ground coriander

Dash of pepper, or to taste

GARNISH (OPTIONAL)   toasted sesame seeds

> **TIP**
>
> Tahini, a paste made of ground sesame seeds, is also called sesame butter. Light tahini is preferable to the more intensely flavored dark tahini, which is made from toasted seeds. Stir before using to incorporate the oil. Store tahini for up to 1 year in a tightly closed container in the refrigerator.

1. Blend the orange juice, tahini, and garlic in a blender until smooth. Add water, as needed, to reach a cake-batter consistency.

2. Pour the mixture into a small nonstick saucepan; add the coriander and pepper. Stir constantly over medium heat, just until the sauce is warm. Adjust the seasoning to taste.

PER TABLESPOON: Cal 82/Prot 3.1g/Carb 2.4g/Fat 6.7g/Chol 0mg/Sod 0mg

ADVANCE PREPARATION   This sauce will keep for up to 2 days in a covered container in the refrigerator. Because it thickens while standing, stir in water, as needed, when reheating.

Variations

*   Add 1 tablespoon poppyseeds.

*   Add 1 tablespoon low-sodium soy sauce.

ginger
sauce

Makes 1 cup

This is an exceptional sauce, not only for the Vegetable Stir-Fry (page 140) and the Batter-Dipped Tofu appetizer (page 34), but also for other stir-fries and steamed vegetables.

6 tablespoons white rice vinegar

6 tablespoons sugar

3/4 cup water

2 tablespoons low-sodium soy sauce

1 tablespoon cold water

1 tablespoon cornstarch

1 tablespoon finely minced fresh ginger
    (see Tip)

TIP

To preserve fresh ginger: Wrap the ginger tightly in aluminum foil or seal it in a small zip-top plastic bag and freeze. When you need ginger, do not thaw; instead, simply use a fine grater to grate off the amount needed. Rewrap and replace immediately in the freezer, where the ginger will keep for up to 3 months.

1. Combine the vinegar, sugar, water, and soy sauce in a small saucepan. Stir constantly over medium-high heat until the mixture comes to a boil. Reduce the heat to medium-low; simmer, stirring occasionally, for 2 minutes.

2. Meanwhile, stir together the cold water and the cornstarch in a small bowl until smooth; stir into the saucepan. Cook, stirring constantly, until the sauce is clear and slightly thickened.

3. Remove the pan from heat; stir in the ginger.

PER TABLESPOON: Cal 23/Prot .1g/Carb 5.4g/Fat 0g/Chol 0mg/Sod 76mg

ADVANCE PREPARATION This sauce will keep for up to 3 days in a covered container in the refrigerator.

peanut
sauce

Makes ³/₄ cup

Poured over warm or chilled vegetables, such as steamed green beans or new potatoes, this sauce will add protein and variety to your meals.

¹/₄ cup smooth peanut butter

¹/₂ cup skim milk

3 tablespoons nonfat plain yogurt

¹/₂ teaspoon dried oregano

¹/₂ teaspoon red pepper flakes

GARNISH (OPTIONAL)   toasted sesame seeds

Stir together all of the ingredients in a small bowl.

PER TABLESPOON: Cal 39/Prot 1.9g/Carb 1.8g/Fat 2.7g/Chol 0mg/Sod 9mg

ADVANCE PREPARATION   This sauce will keep for up to 3 days in a covered container in the refrigerator. Bring to room temperature or gently heat before using. Since it thickens while standing, stir in water as needed when reheating.

chapter 2

Appetizers

LIGHT AND TASTY, THESE APPETIZERS RELY ON FRESH vegetables, herbs, yogurt, and cheeses. Most can be prepared ahead of time and then dished out at the last minute before serving. The best thing about them is that they will satisfy your guests but leave plenty of room for the entrée. And, you'll have time to mingle before dinner. All, especially the Peanut Chili Dip and Cheesy Vegetable Spread, make delicious after-school snacks, so why wait for a party to enjoy them?

almond-mushroom
pâté

Makes 1¹/₂ cups

People who do not like ordinary pâté seem to love this flavorful vegetarian one, especially when it is made with cremini mushrooms instead of ordinary white mushrooms. Serve the intriguing mixture with Pita Crisps (page 63), thick slices of crusty French bread, thin slices of whole wheat bread, or water crackers.

> ## TIP
>
> Cremini mushrooms, sometimes labeled "Italian brown mushrooms," are more flavorful, with a denser, less watery texture than ordinary white mushrooms. Portobello mushrooms are larger, matured cremini mushrooms.

2 tablespoons butter

1¹/₂ cups sliced cremini mushrooms (see Tip)

¹/₄ cup finely chopped onion

1 teaspoon minced garlic

¹/₂ teaspoon dried tarragon

1 cup blanched whole almonds

1 tablespoon fresh lemon juice

2 teaspoons low-sodium soy sauce

Dash of ground white pepper

GARNISH (OPTIONAL)   slivered or finely chopped almonds, pimiento or red bell pepper strips, sprigs of fresh flat-leaf parsley

1. Melt the butter in a large nonstick skillet over medium-high heat. Add the mushrooms, onion, and garlic; cook, stirring occasionally, for about 5 minutes or until the mushrooms are tender. Remove the pan from the heat; stir in the tarragon.

2. Allow the mixture to cool slightly, then transfer it to a food processor. Add the remaining ingredients; process until smooth.

PER TABLESPOON: Cal 54/Prot 1.9g/Carb 1.9g/Fat 4.3g/Chol 3mg/Sod 27mg

ADVANCE PREPARATION   For the best flavor, make this pâté the day before serving. It will keep for up to 4 days in a covered container in the refrigerator. Bring to room temperature before serving.

baba
ghannouj

Makes 2 cups

Plan ahead when making Baba Ghannouj because the flavor improves if it is made a day or so in advance. Serve it chilled or at room temperature as a dip for raw vegetables, or as a spread for sandwiches or Pita Crisps (page 63).

1 medium eggplant (about 12 ounces), peeled and cut into $1/2$-inch cubes (about 3 cups); (see Tips)

$1/4$ cup tahini

1 tablespoon fresh lemon juice

$1/2$ teaspoon minced garlic

$1/4$ teaspoon pepper, or to taste

Dash of ground cumin

2 tablespoons sesame seeds, preferably toasted (see Tips)

2 tablespoons minced fresh flat-leaf parsley

> ### TIPS
>
> - Smaller eggplants have thinner peels and a sweeter flavor. Select those with firm skin free of soft spots.
>
> - Store sesame seeds in an airtight container in the refrigerator for up to 6 months or in the freezer for up to 1 year.

GARNISH (OPTIONAL)   sprigs of fresh flat-leaf parsley

1. Put the eggplant in a microwave-proof dish; add about $1/4$ cup water. Cover and microwave on high for about 5 minutes or until tender. (Or cook the eggplant for about 5 minutes in a stovetop steamer.) Drain well.

2. Transfer the cooked eggplant to a food processor. Add the tahini, lemon juice, and garlic; process until smooth. Stir in the remaining ingredients. Adjust the seasoning to taste.

PER TABLESPOON: Cal 20/Prot .7g/Carb .9g/Fat 1.5g/Chol 0mg/Sod 1mg

ADVANCE PREPARATION   This spread will keep for up to 2 days in a covered container in the refrigerator.

Hummus on cucumber rounds with tomatoes

hummus

Makes 1¹/₂ cups

The popularity of this versatile spread is no surprise. I like to serve it on cucumber rounds, garnished with halved cherry tomatoes and sprigs of flat-leaf parsley. Or use it as a spread for bread or crackers, as a dip, or in pita sandwiches.

1 tablespoon canola or safflower oil

2 tablespoons finely chopped onion

¹/₂ teaspoon minced garlic

¹/₄ cup minced fresh flat-leaf parsley

1 teaspoon dried basil

¹/₄ teaspoon ground coriander (see Tips)

¹/₄ teaspoon dried oregano

¹/₄ teaspoon pepper, or to taste

Dash of ground cumin

1 (15-ounce) can garbanzo beans, drained and rinsed (1¹/₂ cups)

3 tablespoons fresh lemon juice, or as needed

2 tablespoons toasted sesame seeds (see Tips)

GARNISH (OPTIONAL)   lemon wedges, cherry tomatoes, sprigs of fresh flat-leaf parsley

1. Heat the oil in a small nonstick skillet over medium-high heat; add the onion and garlic. Cook, stirring occasionally, for about 2 minutes or until the onion and garlic are softened. Remove from the heat; add the parsley, basil, coriander, oregano, pepper, and cumin. Stir just long enough to soften the parsley.

2. Process the garbanzo beans and lemon juice in a food processor until smooth. Add extra lemon juice as needed so the mixture is spreadable. Add to the onion mixture; stir in the sesame seeds. Adjust the seasoning to taste.

PER TABLESPOON: Cal 43/Prot 1.8g/Carb 5.8g/Fat 1.4/Chol 0mg/Sod 2mg

ADVANCE PREPARATION   The flavor of this spread improves if the mixture is made 1 or 2 days in advance; cover and refrigerate. It will keep for up to 4 days. Bring to room temperature before serving.

TIPS

- Ground coriander is the ground seeds of the cilantro plant. The flavor bears no resemblance to fresh cilantro leaves.

- Toasting gives sesame seeds a slightly crispy texture and a nutty flavor. To toast sesame seeds: Put them in a dry skillet over medium-high heat; toss or stir constantly about 3 to 5 minutes or until they are lightly browned. It takes the same amount of time to toast 1 tablespoon as $1/2$ cup, so toast extra seeds and store them in an airtight container in the refrigerator or freezer.

Variation

- Substitute 1 (15-ounce) can great Northern beans for the garbanzo beans; reduce the lemon juice to 2 tablespoons.

cheesy
vegetable
spread

Makes 1¹/₂ cups

For a snack or appetizer, spread this colorful mixture on Pita Crisps (page 63) or whole wheat bread. And the kids will enjoy its sweet flavor and crunchy texture in their lunch box sandwiches.

1 cup shredded farmer cheese (see Tip)	2 tablespoons finely chopped celery
3 tablespoons nonfat plain yogurt	2 tablespoons finely chopped pecans
1 teaspoon fresh lemon juice	2 tablespoons currants
1 teaspoon low-sodium soy sauce	1 tablespoon toasted wheat germ
¹/₄ cup finely chopped apple	¹/₂ teaspoon curry powder
¹/₄ cup finely chopped carrot	

Process the cheese, yogurt, lemon juice, and soy sauce in a food processor until the mixture is smooth. Stir in the remaining ingredients.

PER TABLESPOON: Cal 20/Prot 1.5/Carb 1.9g/Fat 1.3g/Chol 3mg/Sod 24mg

ADVANCE PREPARATION   This spread will keep for up to 4 days in a covered container in the refrigerator.

Variations

- Substitute Cheddar cheese for the farmer cheese.

- Substitute mayonnaise for the yogurt.

> **TIP**
>
> Farmer cheese is a form of cottage cheese, in which most of the liquid is pressed. The slightly tangy flavor makes it delicious eating as is or when used in cooking.

batter-dipped
tofu

Makes 6 servings

Even "tofu skeptics" will enjoy this nutritious, high-protein appetizer. Or cut the tofu into larger pieces and serve them as an entrée, topped with Vegetable Stir-Fry with Ginger Sauce (page 140).

1 cup Ginger Sauce (page 24)

4 leaves red leaf lettuce

$1/2$ cup all-purpose flour

2 tablespoons toasted wheat germ (see Tips)

$1/2$ teaspoon dried thyme

$1/4$ teaspoon dried dill

$1/4$ teaspoon paprika

$1/4$ teaspoon pepper

1 large egg

1 tablespoon skim milk

$1/4$ teaspoon hot pepper sauce

8 ounces extra-firm or firm tofu, cut into 1-inch squares about $1/2$-inch thick (see Tips)

2 tablespoons canola or safflower oil

1. Prepare the Ginger Sauce; cover and set aside.

2. Arrange the lettuce leaves on a serving plate; set aside.

3. Combine the flour, wheat germ, thyme, dill, paprika, and pepper in a small shallow bowl.

4. Lightly beat the egg in a separate shallow bowl. Stir in the milk and hot pepper sauce.

5. One at a time, gently press the tofu cubes into the flour mixture, covering all sides; dip into the egg mixture and again into the flour mixture. As the cubes are prepared, place them in a single layer on a plate.

6. Heat the oil in a large nonstick skillet over medium-high heat. Place the cubes in a single layer in the skillet; cook for about 3 minutes, or until lightly browned, on each side.

7. To serve, arrange the browned tofu cubes atop the lettuce. Pour the warm Ginger Sauce into a small bowl. Provide cocktail forks for dipping the tofu cubes into the sauce.

PER SERVING: Cal 186/Prot 6.1g/Carb 25g/Fat 6.8g/Chol 35mg/Sod 228mg

ADVANCE PREPARATION   Combine the dry ingredients and the egg-milk mixture early in the day; cover and refrigerate the liquid. For best results, sauté the tofu just before serving.

Variation

- Substitute Zesty Tomato Sauce (page 20) or Sweet and Sour Sauce (page 136) for the Ginger Sauce.

TIPS

- Toasted wheat germ, found in the cereal aisle of most supermarkets, is preferable to raw wheat germ in most recipes because of its nutty flavor and crunchy texture. To prevent rancidity, store it for up to 6 months in a tightly closed container in the refrigerator.

- Tofu is available in several varieties, which vary in water content and are suited to different uses in cooking. Extra-firm and firm tofus are dense and solid; both hold up well when sliced or cubed. Soft tofu is the best choice for recipes that call for puréeing, such as blender drinks, dips, dressings, or soups; the extra liquid it contains yields a smooth and creamy texture. If you do not use the entire package of tofu, store what remains, immersed in water in a refrigerator container, for up to 3 days.

curried
cheese spread
with chutney

Makes 1 cup cheese spread plus chutney

Serve this with crackers or Pita Crisps (page 63) as an appetizer or snack when your time is short but you want to serve something unusual. If you don't have homemade chutney on hand, commercially prepared chutney will do.

1 cup shredded Cheddar cheese

3/4 cup low-fat cream cheese

2 teaspoons curry powder

1 cup Mixed Fruit Chutney (page 15)

2 medium scallions, finely chopped

1. Process the Cheddar cheese, cream cheese, and curry powder in a food processor until the mixture is smooth.

2. Spread the cheese mixture in a 6-inch round serving dish. Spread with a layer of chutney, and sprinkle with chopped scallions.

PER TABLESPOON: Cal 44/Prot 1.5g/Carb 5g/Fat 2/Chol 7mg/Sod 49mg

ADVANCE PREPARATION   This spread will keep for up to 2 days in a covered container in the refrigerator.

Variation

• Stuff the puréed cheese mixture into hollowed-out cherry tomatoes or celery sticks; garnish with minced flat-leaf parsley.

peanut
chili dip

Makes ²/₃ cup

Add a dash of red pepper flakes or cayenne pepper to this dip if you like your food spicy. Serve it with a variety of fresh vegetables, such as carrots, broccoli, green or red bell peppers, or cauliflower.

¹/₃ cup peanut butter (smooth or crunchy); (see Tip)

3 tablespoons water, or as needed

2 tablespoons low-sodium soy sauce

2 tablespoons fresh lemon juice

2 teaspoons honey

1 teaspoon minced garlic

1 tablespoon chili powder

Dash of red pepper flakes or cayenne pepper (optional)

> **TIP**
>
> Buy natural peanut butter with the oil on top; stir in the oil before using. Avoid processed peanut butters that have added stabilizers or sweeteners.

GARNISH (OPTIONAL)   dash of paprika, finely chopped peanuts

Combine the peanut butter and water in a small bowl; add water as needed to make a smooth, creamy paste. Stir in the remaining ingredients.

PER TABLESPOON: Cal 68/Prot 2.5/Carb 4.6g/Fat 4.4g/Chol 0mg/Sod 130mg

ADVANCE PREPARATION   The flavors in this dip will blend if it is made at least several hours in advance; it will keep for up to 5 days in a covered container in the refrigerator.

curried
yogurt
dip

Makes 1 cup

*This is one of my favorite "skinny dips"—rich-tasting and flavorful without the
calories of sour cream. Serve this with your choice of fresh vegetables or Pita
Crisps (page 63).*

3/4 cup nonfat plain yogurt	1/2 teaspoon honey
2 teaspoons curry powder	1/4 teaspoon pepper
1 teaspoon fresh lemon juice	Dash of hot pepper sauce, or to taste

GARNISH (OPTIONAL)   finely chopped almonds or walnuts

Stir together all of the ingredients in a small bowl; adjust the seasoning to taste.

PER TABLESPOON: Cal 7/Prot .6g/Carb 1.2g/Fat 0g/Chol 0mg/Sod 7mg

ADVANCE PREPARATION   This dip can be served immediately, but chilling
for several hours will allow the flavors to develop and blend. It will keep for
up to 3 days in a covered container in the refrigerator.

chapter 3
Soups

NOTHING CAN COMPARE TO HOMEMADE SOUP'S

aroma, flavor, and quality—and it's easy to make. I serve

my soups piping hot from a stainless steel-lined copper

stock pot into heated bowls (I run them through the rinse

cycle of my dishwasher right before serving). Cold soups

are best ladled into bowls chilled in the refrigerator.

Traditionally, creamy soups are thickened with a roux—a cooked mixture of flour and butter to which cream is added. However, when certain cooked vegetables, such as potatoes and peas, are puréed, they can create the same creamy texture (or "mouth feel") with a fraction of the calories and fat. Your blender will get the job done to perfection in seconds; or you can use your food processor, if necessary.

I have suggested garnishes for each soup because I think they are important for adding visual appeal, a flavor complement, and texture. The garnish can be simple, such as a light sprinkling of chopped fresh herbs, finely chopped vegetables, grated cheese, sunflower seeds, nuts, or chopped egg. Or, if you have the time, prepare some Herbed Garlic Croutons (page 64).

While many of my lighter soups make a delicious first course, others are hearty enough to stand on their own as an entrée. Accompany them with Pita Crisps (page 63), Almond Butter-Wheat Germ Sticks (page 61), crusty bread, muffins, or crackers; perhaps a cheese platter; and a tossed green salad.

Asian Stew (page 42)

asian stew

Makes 6 servings

This is an attractive, elegant, low-calorie soup. It's adaptable to many tasty variations, using a wide variety of vegetables. Just before serving, stir in 1 teaspoon of dark sesame oil to add a nutty flavor or a dash of red pepper flakes to add spiciness.

5 cups vegetable stock (see pages xxiv and 3)

1 small onion, thinly sliced, or 2 medium scallions, coarsely chopped

1 teaspoon minced garlic

1 tablespoon minced fresh ginger

2 tablespoons low-sodium soy sauce

3 ribs bok choy, diagonally sliced (also shred green tops)

1 cup broccoli florets

1 red bell pepper, julienned (see Tips)

1 carrot, coarsely shredded

1 cup sliced mushrooms

$1/2$ cup frozen peas (preferably baby peas), thawed

2 ounces thin buckwheat (soba) noodles, broken into 1-inch-long pieces ($1/2$ cup)

8 ounces firm tofu, cut into $1/2$-inch cubes

$1/4$ cup fresh watercress leaves

Dash of white ground pepper, or to taste

GARNISH (OPTIONAL)   blanched stemmed snow peas (see Tips), thin scallion slices, celery or watercress leaves, toasted sesame seeds

1.   Bring $1/2$ cup of the vegetable stock to a boil in a Dutch oven or $3^1/2$- to 5-quart saucepan over medium-high heat. Add the onion, garlic, and ginger; cover and cook for 3 minutes.

2. Stir in the remaining stock and soy sauce; cover and bring to a boil. Add the remaining ingredients as they are prepared. Cover and cook, stirring occasionally, for about 8 minutes or until the noodles are tender (the vegetables remain crisp-tender). Adjust the seasoning to taste.

PER SERVING: Cal 91/Prot 6.4g/Carb 13.3g/Fat 1.4g/Chol 0mg/Sod 253mg

ADVANCE PREPARATION   This soup will keep for up to 3 days in a covered container in the refrigerator. Take care not to overcook the vegetables when reheating.

Variations

- Substitute other vegetables (up to 5 cups total). Try coarsely chopped water chestnuts, coarsely chopped jicama, shredded stemmed spinach leaves, or bamboo shoots.

- Substitute 1 cup cooked brown rice for the buckwheat noodles.

- To add protein, stir Egg Threads (see Tips) into the soup just before serving.

TIPS

- "Julienne" refers to cutting foods into thin, about 1/8-inch-wide, matchstick strips.

- "Blanching" means to plunge food quickly into simmering water and then immediately into cold water to stop the cooking. Blanching enhances the colors and flavors of vegetables and also loosens the skins of tomatoes, peaches, and nuts (such as almonds), making them easy to peel.

- To make Egg Threads: Heat about 1 teaspoon butter in a small skillet over medium-high heat. When it begins to bubble, add 1 egg beaten with a little cold water. Tilt the pan so the egg mixture coats it in a thin layer, the thinner the better. When the egg is lightly cooked, turn it out onto a cutting board. Use a sharp knife to slice the cooked egg into very thin strips. Makes about 1/3 cup.

meatless
mission
chili

Makes 4 servings

This is a meatless adaptation of one of our old favorites. In fall or winter, it's a satisfying entrée, served with homemade corn bread and a crisp green salad on the side. Everyone especially likes the raw cashews (see Variations).

2 tablespoons canola or safflower oil

1 green bell pepper, coarsely chopped

1 carrot, coarsely shredded

1 small zucchini, coarsely shredded

1 rib celery, coarsely chopped

1/4 cup coarsely chopped onion

1/2 teaspoon minced garlic

1 (18-ounce) can tomatoes, with juice

1 (15-ounce) can kidney beans, drained and rinsed (1 3/4 cups)

1 (8-ounce) can tomato sauce

1/4 cup water

1 1/2 teaspoons chili powder, or to taste

1/4 teaspoon hot pepper sauce, or to taste (see Tip)

1 teaspoon dried basil

1 teaspoon dried oregano

1/2 teaspoon pepper, or to taste

GARNISH (OPTIONAL)   corn, coarsely chopped scallions, shredded Cheddar or Monterey Jack cheese

1. Heat the oil in a Dutch oven or 3 1/2- to 5-quart saucepan over medium-high heat. Add the bell pepper, carrot, zucchini, celery, onion, and garlic; cook, stirring occasionally, for about 3 minutes or until crisp-tender.

2. Stir in the remaining ingredients. When the liquid comes to a boil, reduce the heat to medium. Cover and cook for about 5 minutes or until the chili is heated through. Adjust the seasonings to taste.

PER SERVING: Cal 250/Prot 10g/Carb 35g/Fat 7.7g/Chol 0mg/Sod 436mg

ADVANCE PREPARATION   This soup will keep for up to 4 days in a covered container in the refrigerator. Because it thickens while standing, stir in extra liquid (water, vegetable stock, or tomato juice) as needed when reheating.

> ## TIP
>
> Refrigerate hot pepper sauce after opening to retain its flavor and red color.

Variations

- When adding the tomatoes and beans, also add: $1/2$ cup whole raw cashews or 8 ounces firm tofu, cut into $1/2$-inch cubes.

- As the chili is heating, stir in 1 cup corn (either canned or frozen).

- Just before serving, sprinkle each serving with shredded cheese; heat under the broiler just until the cheese is melted.

quick
pea
soup

Makes 6 servings

This thick, robust soup is a snap to prepare using a blender or food processor. For a vivid green color, use frozen baby peas, rather than the larger, mature variety.

2 tablespoons butter

1/2 cup coarsely chopped onion

2 ribs celery, finely chopped

1 teaspoon minced garlic

2 cups vegetable stock (see pages xxiv and 3)

1 (16-ounce) bag frozen peas (preferably baby peas), thawed

Dash of ground white pepper, or to taste

1/2 cup skim milk

Dash of nutmeg (preferably freshly grated); (see Tip)

GARNISH (OPTIONAL)   1/4 cup minced fresh flat-leaf parsley combined with 2 tablespoons finely grated lemon peel, freshly grated Parmesan cheese, Herbed Garlic Croutons (page 64)

1. Melt the butter in a Dutch oven or 3 1/2- to 5-quart saucepan over medium-high heat. Add the onion, celery, and garlic. Cook, stirring occasionally, for about 5 minutes or until tender. Stir in the vegetable stock, peas, and white pepper. Reduce the heat to medium; cook, stirring occasionally, for about 5 minutes.

2. Transfer the mixture (in 2 batches) to a blender or food processor; process until smooth.

3. Return the mixture to the pan; add the milk and nutmeg. Stir constantly until the mixture is heated through. Adjust the seasoning to taste.

PER SERVING: Cal 118/Prot 5.2g/Carb 14.4g/Fat 4.4g/Chol 11mg/Sod 133mg

ADVANCE PREPARATION   This soup will keep for up to 3 days in a covered container in the refrigerator. If you prefer, refrigerate the puréed vegetable mixture for up to 3 days; heat the mixture and complete the recipe just before serving.

Variation

•   When heating the soup before serving, stir in $1/2$ cup cooked sliced carrot or $1/2$ cup sautéed sliced mushrooms.

> **TIP**
>
> Freshly grated whole nutmeg is more aromatic and flavorful than preground nutmeg. Use a nutmeg grater, which can be purchased in a gourmet shop. Whole nutmeg will keep its flavor for years if stored in a jar in your spice cabinet.

puréed
vegetable soup
with **broccoli florets**

Makes 4 servings

The thickener in this soup is puréed potatoes, eliminating the need for the cream, butter, and flour found in most cream soups. The texture is quite thick; add more milk, vegetable stock, or water if you prefer a thinner soup.

2 cups vegetable stock (see pages xxiv and 3)

2 potatoes, peeled and diced (about 2 cups)

2 carrots, finely chopped

2 ribs celery, finely chopped

$1/4$ cup finely chopped onion

$1/2$ teaspoon minced garlic

$1/2$ teaspoon dried thyme

$1/4$ teaspoon pepper, or to taste

Dash of nutmeg (preferably freshly grated)

3 cups broccoli florets

1 cup skim milk (see Tips)

1 egg yolk, lightly beaten (see Tips)

1 tablespoon low-sodium soy sauce

GARNISH (OPTIONAL)   dash of paprika, minced fresh flat-leaf parsley or chives, shredded cheese, or diced red bell pepper

1. Put the vegetable stock, potatoes, carrots, celery, onion, garlic, thyme, pepper, and nutmeg into a Dutch oven or $3^{1}/2$- to 5-quart saucepan over medium-high heat. When the liquid comes to a boil, reduce the heat to medium and cook for about 10 minutes or until vegetables are very tender. (The potatoes must be fully cooked to thicken the soup properly.)

2. While the soup is cooking, steam the broccoli florets. Put them into a microwave-proof dish; add about $^1/_4$ cup water. Cover and microwave on high for about 5 minutes or until tender. (Or cook the broccoli for about 5 minutes in a stovetop steamer.) Drain well. Also stir together the milk, egg yolk, and soy sauce in a measuring cup; set aside.

3. When the potatoes are tender, transfer the soup mixture to a blender (in 2 batches); process until completely smooth.

4. Return the puréed soup to the pan. Add the broccoli florets and the milk mixture. Stir the soup constantly over medium heat until heated through; do not allow it to boil. Adjust the seasoning to taste.

PER SERVING: Cal 181/Prot 8.4g/Carb 33.3g/Fat 1.6g/Chol 54mg/Sod 258mg

ADVANCE PREPARATION   This soup will keep for up to 3 days in a covered container in the refrigerator. When reheating, do not allow the soup to come to a boil. If you prefer, refrigerate the puréed vegetable mixture for up to 3 days; heat the mixture and complete the recipe just before serving.

Variations

• Substitute 2 cups steamed sliced carrots or 2 cups frozen peas, or a combination of both, for the steamed broccoli florets.

• Add 1 cup shredded Cheddar cheese and melt it into the soup base before adding the broccoli florets; substitute a pinch of powdered mustard for the nutmeg.

> ## TIPS
>
> • Dissolving $^1/_4$ cup milk powder per cup of milk will provide added calcium and protein without altering the flavor of soups and sauces calling for milk.
>
> • To add egg yolks to a hot mixture, combine a small amount of the hot mixture with the egg in a small bowl, then gradually stir it into the hot mixture over low heat. Do not allow the mixture to come to a boil because it may curdle.

winter
carrot
soup

Makes 6 servings

Your fussiest eaters will love this soup. Fortunately, the ingredients are staples you are likely to have on hand and it's a breeze to make. Serve with sliced cheese and Pita Crisps (page 63) for a quick winter lunch.

1 tablespoon canola or safflower oil	1 (6-ounce) can tomato paste
4 carrots, coarsely grated	1 tablespoon low-sodium soy sauce
1/2 cup coarsely chopped onion (see Tips)	1/2 teaspoon dried thyme
4 cups vegetable stock (see pages xxiv and 3)	1/4 teaspoon ground cumin
	1/4 teaspoon pepper, or to taste

GARNISH (OPTIONAL)   Herbed Garlic Croutons (page 64)

1. Heat the oil in a Dutch oven or 3 1/2- to 5-quart saucepan over medium-high heat. Add the carrots and onion; cook, stirring occasionally, for about 5 minutes or until tender.

2. Combine 1 cup of the stock and the tomato paste in a measuring cup; whisk until smooth. Add to the pot with the remaining ingredients. Cover and increase the heat to high. When the liquid begins to boil, reduce heat to medium and cook for about 5 minutes. Adjust the seasoning to taste.

PER SERVING: Cal 84/Prot 2g/Carb 13.2g/Fat 2.6g/Chol 0mg/Sod 147mg

ADVANCE PREPARATION   This soup will keep for up to 4 days in a covered container in the refrigerator.

Variation

- When stirring in the stock, add one of the following: $^{1}/_{2}$ cup chopped apple, cooked brown rice, or raw cashews.

TIPS

- Onions will keep for up to 2 months if stored in a cool, dry, and dark place with good air circulation. If you prefer, refrigerate them for up to 1 week.

- Tear-producing vapors can be reduced by refrigerating an onion for several hours or freezing it for 20 minutes before chopping.

- If you chop onions by hand, rub your hands with lemon or celery, then wash to remove the odor.

pasta
and **bean**
soup

Makes 4 servings

This hearty meal-in-a-bowl contains legumes (chickpeas and kidney beans) and a grain (pasta), which combine to form a complete protein. Vary the soup by substituting other vegetables, beans, or pasta shape.

1 tablespoon olive oil

$^1/_2$ cup coarsely chopped onion

$^1/_2$ green bell pepper, coarsely chopped

$^1/_2$ teaspoon minced garlic

4 cups vegetable stock (see pages xxiv and 3) or water

1 (6-ounce) can tomato paste

1 (15-ounce) can chickpeas, drained and rinsed ($1^1/_2$ cups)

1 (15-ounce) can kidney beans, drained and rinsed ($1^1/_2$ cups)

1 teaspoon dried thyme

$^1/_2$ teaspoon dried summer savory

$^3/_4$ teaspoon pepper, or to taste

Dash of cayenne pepper, or to taste

$^1/_2$ cup elbow macaroni, small shells, or spaghetti broken into 1-inch lengths

GARNISH (OPTIONAL)   freshly grated Parmesan cheese

1. Heat the oil in a Dutch oven or $3^1/_2$- to 5-quart saucepan over medium-high heat. Add the onion, bell pepper, and garlic; cook, stirring occasionally for about 5 minutes or until tender.

2. Stir in the remaining ingredients, except the pasta; increase the heat to high. When the liquid begins to boil, stir in the pasta. Reduce the heat to medium. Cover and cook for about 6 minutes or until the pasta is tender. Adjust the seasonings to taste.

PER SERVING: Cal 305/Prot 13.9g/Carb 48.9g/Fat 6g/Chol 5mg/Sod 450mg

ADVANCE PREPARATION   This soup will keep for up to 3 days in a covered container in the refrigerator. Because it thickens while standing, add water as needed when reheating.

Variations

- Add other vegetables (up to 1 cup total). Try chopped red bell pepper, broccoli florets, or sliced mushrooms.

- To make minestrone: Add $1/2$ cup coarsely chopped carrot when cooking the bell pepper; substitute 1 teaspoon dried basil and 1 teaspoon dried oregano for the savory, thyme, and cayenne pepper.

- To serve as a skillet main course, add only 1 cup vegetable stock or water; or use 3 cups vegetable stock and increase the pasta to 1 cup.

moroccan
chickpea
soup

Makes 4 servings

Chickpeas are the same as garbanzo beans; and they are sometimes called ceci beans.

2 tablespoons canola or safflower oil

2 carrots, coarsely grated

$1/2$ cup finely chopped onion

1 teaspoon minced garlic

1 (15-ounce) can chickpeas, drained and rinsed ($1^1/2$ cups)

3 cups vegetable stock (see pages xxiv and 3)

$1/3$ cup tahini

2 tablespoons fresh lemon juice (see Tips)

1 tablespoon minced fresh flat-leaf parsley

$3/4$ teaspoon ground cumin

$1/2$ teaspoon pepper, or to taste

$1/2$ teaspoon dried thyme

$1/4$ teaspoon turmeric

$1/8$ teaspoon cayenne pepper, or to taste

GARNISH (OPTIONAL)   toasted sesame seeds, minced scallions, finely chopped tomatoes, Herbed Garlic Croutons (page 64)

1. Heat the oil in a Dutch oven or $3^1/2$- to 5-quart saucepan over medium-high heat. Add the carrots, onion, and garlic; cook, stirring occasionally, until tender. Set aside.

2. Meanwhile, process the chickpeas, 1 cup of the vegetable stock, tahini, and lemon juice in a food processor until smooth.

3. Stir the puréed mixture into the pan, then add the remaining vegetable stock and the other ingredients. Cover and cook, stirring occasionally, for about 5 minutes or until heated through. Adjust the seasonings to taste.

PER SERVING: Cal 306/Prot 11.2g/Carb 39.6g/Fat 11.4g/Chol 0mg/Sod 29mg

ADVANCE PREPARATION   This soup will keep for up to 4 days in a covered container in the refrigerator. Because it thickens while standing, stir in water as needed when reheating.

Variations

• Substitute olive oil for canola or safflower oil.

• Add $1/2$ cup finely chopped red bell pepper; sauté with the vegetables.

TIPS

• Freshly squeezed citrus juice is always the most flavorful. Avoid chemical-laden and artificial-tasting reconstituted lemon and lime juice.

• To squeeze more juice from citrus fruits, first bring them to room temperature; or microwave chilled fruit (pierce the fruit with a fork or knife first) for 30 seconds on high. Then roll the fruit on a hard surface, pressing hard with the palm of your hand for a minute or so, to break the inner membranes.

chunky
garden gazpacho

Makes 6 servings

This full-flavored soup of Spanish origin needs no cooking—a welcome treat during the hot summer months. For a do-ahead summer lunch, accompany it with the Couscous-Currant Salad with Lemon Dressing (page 96).

1 (15-ounce) can tomato sauce	1 rib celery, coarsely chopped
2 tablespoons extra-virgin olive oil	1/2 teaspoon minced garlic
2 tablespoons red wine vinegar (see Tip)	1 medium scallion, coarsely chopped
1 tablespoon honey	1/2 cucumber, seeded and coarsely chopped
1 tomato, cut into 1/2-inch cubes	
1 green bell pepper, coarsely chopped	1/2 teaspoon hot pepper sauce, or to taste
1 red bell pepper, coarsely chopped	1/2 teaspoon pepper, or to taste

GARNISH (OPTIONAL)   Herbed Garlic Croutons (page 64), dollops of plain yogurt topped with finely minced fresh chives, sprigs of fresh flat-leaf parsley

Combine the tomato sauce, olive oil, vinegar, and honey in a medium bowl. Stir in the remaining ingredients. Adjust the seasonings to taste.

PER SERVING: Cal 100/Prot 1.7g/Carb 12.4g/Fat 4.8g/Chol 0mg/Sod 438mg

ADVANCE PREPARATION   This soup will keep for up to 4 days in a covered container in the refrigerator. Because it thickens while standing, thin by stirring in water or tomato juice as needed.

Variation

• For a smoother texture, purée the completed soup in a blender.

> **TIP**
>
> Most vinegars will keep for up to 2 years without refrigeration. Some, especially red wine vinegar, may become cloudy or develop a sediment. If this happens, the flavor will not be affected, and the liquid can be cleared by running it through a paper coffee filter.

Strawberry Soup

strawberry
soup

Makes 4 servings

This chilled soup is one of my summer favorites when strawberries are at their ripest and sweetest.

1 cup nonfat plain yogurt

1 cup sliced fresh strawberries

2 tablespoons fresh orange juice

1 tablespoon honey

GARNISH (OPTIONAL)   fresh strawberry or kiwi slices, sprigs of fresh mint

Process all of the ingredients in a blender until smooth and creamy.

PER SERVING: Cal 124/Prot 3.6g/Carb 25.6g/Fat .8g/Chol 1mg/Sod 38mg

ADVANCE PREPARATION   This soup will keep for up to 2 days in a covered container in the refrigerator.

Variation

• Substitute white or red grape juice or apple juice for orange juice.

blueberry
soup

Makes 4 servings

I nearly always prefer using fresh fruit, but this soup is actually best when made with frozen blueberries. Keep some on hand so you can surprise your family with this special treat.

2 cups nonfat plain yogurt

2 cups fresh orange juice

1 tablespoon honey

$1/2$ teaspoon ground cinnamon

1 cup frozen unsweetened blueberries, thawed

GARNISH (OPTIONAL)   sprigs of fresh mint

Combine all of the ingredients, except the blueberries, in a blender; process until smooth and creamy. Stir in the blueberries.

PER SERVING: Cal 152/Prot 7g/Carb 30g/Fat .5g/Chol 3mg/Sod 77mg

ADVANCE PREPARATION   This soup will keep for up to 2 days in a covered container in the refrigerator.

almond
butter-wheat germ
sticks

Makes 16 sticks

These toasted bread strips are an out-of-the-ordinary soup accompaniment or do-ahead appetizer; they also make a tasty lunch box surprise. If you don't have almond butter, substitute creamy peanut butter.

4 slices firm whole wheat bread

$^1/_3$ cup roasted almond butter (see Tip)

2 tablespoons canola or safflower oil, or as needed

$^1/_4$ cup toasted wheat germ

1. Preheat the oven to 350°F.

2. Trim the crusts from the bread slices; cut each slice into 4 strips. Arrange the strips on a baking sheet. Toast in the oven for 5 minutes on each side or until lightly browned and crispy.

3. Meanwhile, heat the almond butter and oil in a small nonstick saucepan, stirring occasionally, until it is thinned and smooth. (The amount of oil needed may vary according to the consistency of almond butter.)

4. Pour the wheat germ into a shallow bowl. Dip both sides of each toasted bread strip into the warm almond butter; then press each side into the wheat germ. Let stand on a baking sheet for a few minutes or until dry.

PER SERVING (2 STICKS): Cal 180/Prot 4.5g/Carb 15.5g/Fat 11.1g/Chol 0mg/Sod 81mg

(continues)

ADVANCE PREPARATION   These toast strips will keep for up to 2 days in a tightly closed container in the refrigerator.

Variations

• Substitute cashew butter for the almond butter, or use a combination.

• Add 1 tablespoon honey when heating the almond butter or peanut butter.

TIP

Roasted almond butter, a product similar to peanut butter, is made from puréed almonds; you'll find it in natural food stores and some supermarkets.

pita
crisps

Makes 4 servings

Serve these as an appetizer or snack or as a crispy accompaniment to soups or salads. They are at their best when prepared just before serving.

2 (6-inch) pita breads

2 teaspoons butter

$^{1}/_{4}$ cup freshly grated Parmesan cheese

2 teaspoons dried oregano

1. Position the oven broiler rack 4 to 5 inches from the heating element; preheat the broiler.

2. Split the pitas horizontally into 2 rounds. Place the halves on an ungreased baking sheet, rough sides up. Lightly spread them with butter.

3. Toss together the Parmesan cheese and oregano in a small bowl. Sprinkle over the butter. Use kitchen shears to cut each pita half into 6 wedges.

4. Broil for about 2 minutes or until the wedges are lightly browned and the cheese is melted. Watch closely! (The wedges will become more crispy as they cool.)

PER SERVING: Cal 125/Prot 4.9g/Carb 17.4g/Fat 4g/Chol 9mg/Sod 275mg

Variation

• Substitute other dried herbs, such as basil or tarragon, for the oregano.

herbed garlic
croutons

Makes 2 cups

These croutons are the "little extra" that adds flavor to soups and salads. They also provide a pleasing contrast to the smooth texture of creamy soups.

2 tablespoons butter,
  preferably unsalted

1 teaspoon minced garlic

$1/2$ teaspoon dried basil

$1/2$ teaspoon dried oregano

2 cups $1/2$-inch bread cubes, preferably
  whole wheat (see Tip)

1. Melt the butter in a large nonstick skillet over medium heat. Add the garlic, basil, and oregano; stir constantly for about 30 seconds to soften the herbs. Increase the heat to medium-high. Add the bread cubes; stir for about 4 to 5 minutes or until lightly browned and crispy.

2. Transfer the croutons to a plate and set aside to cool. (The croutons will become crisper as they cool.)

PER SERVING: Cal 83/Prot 1.4g/Carb 8.3g/Fat 4.9g/Chol 11mg/Sod 54mg

ADVANCE PREPARATION   These croutons can be stored in a covered tin at room temperature for up to 2 days (they become soggy in a covered plastic container). To recrisp (if necessary), spread the croutons in a single layer on a baking sheet and heat at 350°F for about 5 minutes.

Variation

•   Substitute other dried herbs, such as thyme, for the basil and oregano.

chapter 4

Salads

SALADS CAN BE EITHER THE STAR OR THE SUPPORTING

player of a meal. Prepared carefully and arranged artfully,

salads can add many elements to a menu: texture, color,

coolness, and even an ethnic touch. When selecting a

salad to accompany a spicy and hot entrée, choose one

that is cooling. If the entrée is subtle, the salad should be

bold, crunchy, and tart. Pair a simple salad that won't com-

pete for attention with an entrée that is unusual or exotic.

Other salads can make a beautiful, refreshing entrée that will please the heartiest appetite. Many of the salads in this chapter contain protein sources—beans, seeds, nuts, tofu, or cheese—which make them substantial enough to stand on their own.

One of the nicest things about salads is the diversity of ingredients that can be used to make them. Feel free to adapt the recipes to include your favorite ingredients and to use those you may have on hand. The only rule is to always start with the freshest, highest-quality ingredients.

Tossed Green Salads

A simple tossed salad is often a quick-to-prepare accompaniment to a 15-minute entrée. Or, with a little more time and a wider array of ingredients, the salad can be turned into a healthful main course itself. For an informal lunch or dinner, try a make-it-yourself salad bar accompanied by a homemade dressing or two, soup, and a selection of breads. As an added touch, toss salads in a chilled bowl and serve them on chilled plates or bowls.

The success of a green salad depends on fresh greens. Most produce departments now sell many types, varying in texture from crispy to chewy and in flavor from peppery and pungent to sweet. Using an assortment will add interest to your salads.

Before using, wash the greens well under cool running water soon before they are to be used; never allow them to soak in water. After washing, drain and dry the leaves with paper towels or whirl the greens in a salad spinner. Excess water on the greens will dilute the flavor of your dressing and may prevent it from adhering. To avoid brown edges, always tear the lettuce leaves by hand.

As a time saver, chop vegetables for your salad when time permits; refrigerate them in air-tight containers for up to two days.

Although some salads are classics, there are really no rules for making a good salad combination. Salad ingredients can be much more than just lettuce and tomatoes. In the chart at right, are some suggestions for adding variety to your salads; let them inspire your creativity.

THE 15-MINUTE VEGETARIAN SALAD BOWL

Lettuce

bitter: Belgian endive, dandelion greens, curly
    endive (chicory), escarole (broad leaf endive)

chewy: radicchio, mâche

crunchy: romaine, iceberg (head lettuce)

peppery and pungent: arugula, bok choy, Chinese
    cabbage (napa), sorrel, Swiss chard

soft: Bibb, Boston, red leaf

variation (other greens): salad spinach leaves,
    green or red cabbage, kale

Low-Calorie Additions

alfalfa sprouts	cabbage	leeks	snow peas
asparagus	carrots	mushrooms	summer squash
bean sprouts	cauliflower florets	onions	tomatoes
beets	celery	peas	water chestnuts
bell peppers: green, red, orange, yellow	cucumbers	potatoes	zucchini
	green beans	radishes	
broccoli florets	jicama root	scallions	

Protein Additions

beans: garbanzo beans, kidney beans, lentils,
    cheese

eggs: hard-cooked or Egg Threads (page 43)

nuts: best if they are toasted

seeds: best if they are toasted

Miscellaneous Additions

fruit (both fresh and dried): apples, grapes, orange
    sections, strawberries, raisins, dried cranberries

grains: couscous, rice, barley, bulgur wheat

Herbed Garlic Croutons (page 64)

oil-packed sun-dried tomatoes, drained
    pasta

Dressing Salads

Making your own dressings from scratch has the benefit of avoiding the additives and preservatives found in most supermarket dressings. The array of combinations is endless; the time and equipment needed are minimal. It's easiest to make most dressings in a jar with a lid; add all of the ingredients and simply shake. For the best results, follow these simple guidelines:

- Most dressings seem quite strong when tasted from a spoon; instead taste your dressing by dipping a salad ingredient into it.

- Dress bean and grain salads as soon as they are prepared. The flavors will blend if these salads are allowed to stand before serving.

- Leafy green salads will wilt and lose their crispness if dressed more than just a few minutes before they are eaten. Add just enough dressing to coat the ingredients.

To follow are some of my favorite homemade dressings, and those that appear with the salad recipes also have many other uses.

honey-poppyseed
dressing

Makes 1 cup

I nearly always have a container of this dressing on hand in my refrigerator. It's my favorite for serving on green salads or fruit, or the two in tasty combination. Try it on a tossed salad of romaine lettuce, mandarin oranges, celery, raisins, and toasted sliced almonds.

$^{1}/_{3}$ cup white rice vinegar

$^{1}/_{3}$ cup canola or safflower oil (see Tip)

$^{1}/_{3}$ cup honey

1 tablespoon poppyseeds

$^{1}/_{4}$ teaspoon pepper, or to taste

Whisk together all of the ingredients in a small bowl. Adjust the seasoning to taste.

PER TABLESPOON: Cal 67/Prot .1g/Carb 6g/Fat 4.7g/Chol 0mg/Sod 1mg

ADVANCE PREPARATION   This dressing will keep for up to 2 weeks in a tightly closed container in the refrigerator. Whisk or shake before using.

TIP

When recipes call for oil and honey, measure the oil first. Then use the same measuring cup or spoon, without washing, for the honey. It will easily slide out of the cup or spoon.

sesame-soy
dressing

TIPS

- White rice vinegar, made from fermented rice, has a low acidity and is milder and sweeter than ordinary white vinegar. It can be found in Asian markets and in most supermarkets.

- Buy dark, amber-colored sesame oil made from toasted sesame seeds, rather than light-colored sesame oil, which is extracted from raw sesame seeds and lacks the distinctive strong, nutty flavor. Buy it in Asian markets or in the ethnic section of most supermarkets. After opening, store it in the refrigerator, where it will keep for up to 6 months.

Makes $1/2$ cup

This dressing is perfect for salads to accompany your menus with an Asian theme. If you want to make the dressing zesty, add a dash of red pepper flakes or $1/4$ teaspoon Chinese hot oil.

$1/3$ cup white rice vinegar (see Tips)

3 tablespoons dark sesame oil (see Tips)

2 tablespoons low-sodium soy sauce

2 teaspoons minced fresh ginger

2 teaspoons sesame seeds, preferably toasted

3 teaspoons sugar

Dash of ground white pepper, or to taste

Whisk together all of the ingredients in a small bowl, making certain the sugar is dissolved. Adjust the seasoning to taste.

PER TABLESPOON: Cal 111/Prot .4g/Carb 2.5g/Fat 11g/Chol 0mg/Sod 260mg

ADVANCE PREPARATION   This dressing will keep for up to 1 week in a tightly closed container in the refrigerator. Whisk or shake before using.

tangy
honey-mustard
dressing

Makes ½ cup

In addition to being used to spark up a salad, try heating this dressing gently to use as a warm sauce over steamed vegetables, such as steamed asparagus spears. It's especially good when made with the Mayonnaise on page 14.

2 tablespoons mayonnaise

2 tablespoons white rice vinegar

1 tablespoon fresh lemon juice

1 teaspoon Dijon mustard or Mustard (page 13)

1 teaspoon honey (see Tip)

½ teaspoon minced garlic

Dash of ground white pepper, or to taste

Few drops of hot pepper sauce, or to taste

1 medium scallion, minced

1 tablespoon minced fresh flat-leaf parsley

Process all of the ingredients in a food processor or blender until smooth. Adjust the seasonings to taste.

PER TABLESPOON: Cal 18/Prot .2g/Carb 2.4g/Fat .8g/Chol 1mg/Sod 24mg

ADVANCE PREPARATION   This dressing will keep for up to 1 week in a tightly closed container in the refrigerator. It thickens when left standing; thin by stirring in water as needed.

> **TIP**
>
> Store honey at room temperature. If it crystallizes, place the jar in hot water to dissolve the crystals.

basic
vinaigrette

Makes ¹/₂ cup

Vary this basic recipe by using other herbs, such as marjoram, tarragon, thyme, paprika, or celery seed.

¹/₄ cup fresh lemon juice	1 tablespoon dried basil
¹/₄ cup red wine vinegar	1 teaspoon pepper, or to taste
2 tablespoons extra-virgin olive oil	¹/₂ teaspoon dried oregano
1 tablespoon Dijon mustard (see Tip)	¹/₂ teaspoon minced garlic

Whisk together all of the ingredients in a small bowl. Adjust the seasoning to taste.

PER TABLESPOON: Cal 44/Prot .3g/Carb 2.8g/Fat 3.5g/Chol 0mg/Sod 12mg

TIP

Dijon mustard, which originated in Dijon, France, is made from brown mustard seeds, spices, and white wine. It is more flavorful than ordinary yellow ballpark mustard.

ADVANCE PREPARATION   This vinaigrette will keep for up to 1 week in a tightly closed container in the refrigerator. Whisk or shake before using.

Variation

• For sweetness, add honey to taste.

apple
salad
dressing

Makes 1 cup

Serve this low-calorie dressing on tossed green salads, sliced tomatoes, or mixed fruit salads.

$1/2$ cup nonfat plain yogurt

$1/4$ cup frozen apple juice concentrate,
   thawed, not diluted

1 tablespoon fresh lemon juice

1 teaspoon honey

$1/2$ teaspoon celery seeds (see Tip)

$1/4$ teaspoon pepper, or to taste

Stir together all of the ingredients in a small bowl. Adjust the seasoning to taste.

PER TABLESPOON: Cal 14/Prot .4/Carb 3g/Fat 0g/Chol 0mg/Sod 6mg

ADVANCE PREPARATION   This dressing will keep for up to 1 week in a tightly closed container in the refrigerator. Stir before using.

TIP

Celery seeds are the seeds from lovage, a wild celery that comes from India. They have a strong flavor, so use them sparingly.

summer
peach
vinaigrette

Makes ¹/₂ cup

Make this when peaches are at their juicy summer best. Serve it on greens or a bowl of mixed fruit; garnish with fresh blueberries.

1 peach (at room temperature), peeled, pitted, and quartered (see Tip)

¹/₄ cup canola or safflower oil

2 tablespoons fresh lemon juice

2 tablespoons white rice vinegar

Dash of pepper, or to taste

Process all of the ingredients in a food processor or blender until smooth. Adjust the seasoning to taste.

PER TABLESPOON: Cal 72/Prot .1g/Carb 2.5g/Fat 6.8g/Chol 0mg/Sod 0mg

TIP

Avoid very hard peaches with no fragrance. Instead, choose peaches that are firm to slightly soft with a yellow or creamy skin tone. To speed up ripening, put peaches in a paper bag with an apple and let stand at room temperature for 2 to 3 days. When fully ripe, keep peaches in a sealed bag in the refrigerator; use within a few days.

ADVANCE PREPARATION   For the freshest flavor, make this vinaigrette just before serving; it will keep for up to 1 day in a tightly closed container in the refrigerator. Whisk or shake before using.

Variations

- Add a dash of honey or sugar, if needed for sweetness.

- Substitute a nectarine for the peach.

- To make strawberry vinaigrette: Substitute ¹/₂ cup sliced strawberries for the peach, 1 tablespoon orange juice concentrate (thawed, not diluted) for the lemon juice, red wine vinegar for the rice vinegar, and 1 teaspoon sugar for the pepper.

chutney
dressing

Makes 1 cup

*This sweet-tart dressing with a hint of curry is made with either Mixed Fruit Chutney (page 15)
or with chutney purchased at the supermarket.*

$^1/_2$ cup chutney

$^1/_3$ cup canola or safflower oil

$^1/_4$ cup fresh lemon juice

2 tablespoons water

$^1/_4$ teaspoon curry powder, or to taste

Process all of the ingredients in a food processor or blender until smooth. Adjust the
seasoning to taste.

PER TABLESPOON: Cal 57/Prot .2g/Carb 4g/Fat 4.5g/Chol 0mg/Sod 1mg

ADVANCE PREPARATION   This dressing will keep for up to 3 days in a tightly closed container in
the refrigerator. Stir or shake before using.

herbed
tomato
sauce

Makes 1 cup

This simple, uncooked sauce seems to be everyone's favorite for pasta salads. It's also delicious tossed with warm pasta or steamed vegetables, or drizzled over an omelet.

1 (8-ounce) can tomato sauce

2 tablespoons extra-virgin olive oil

1 tablespoon red wine vinegar

1/2 teaspoon minced garlic

1 teaspoon dried basil (see Tips)

1 teaspoon dried oregano (see Tips)

1 teaspoon pepper, or to taste

TIPS

- When stored in a tightly closed tin or glass container (rather than a box) in a dark, dry place, dried herbs will remain flavorful for about 1 year. (It's a good idea to date the containers.) They should resemble the color they were when fresh and should not be brownish-green.

- To get the most flavor out of your dried herbs, crumble them between your fingers to release the aromatics as they are added to your recipes.

Combine all of the ingredients in a small bowl. Adjust the seasoning to taste.

PER TABLESPOON: Cal 22/Prot .3g/Carb 1.4g/Fat 1.7g/Chol 0mg/Sod 93mg

ADVANCE PREPARATION   This sauce will keep for up to 1 week in a tightly closed container in the refrigerator. Stir before using.

Variation

- Add 1/4 cup finely chopped oil-packed sun-dried tomatoes.

yogurt-parmesan
dressing

Makes 1 cup

This dressing adds its tangy flavor to pasta salads. Try it spooned over slices of sweet, juicy beefsteak tomatoes, too.

1 cup nonfat plain yogurt

$1/4$ cup freshly grated Parmesan cheese

1 tablespoon fresh lemon juice

$1/2$ teaspoon minced garlic

1 teaspoon dried dill

1 teaspoon pepper, or to taste

Combine all of the ingredients in a small bowl. Adjust the seasoning to taste.

PER TABLESPOON: Cal 16/Prot 1.4g/Carb 1.5g/Fat.5g/Chol 0mg/Sod 39mg

ADVANCE PREPARATION   This dressing will keep for up to 2 days in a tightly closed container in the refrigerator.

creamy
italian
dressing

Makes 1 cup

This is a low-fat version of the classic.

$1/3$ cup nonfat cottage cheese

$1/3$ cup nonfat plain yogurt (see Tip)

2 tablespoons extra-virgin olive oil

2 tablespoons minced onion

$1/2$ teaspoon minced garlic

1 tablespoon fresh lemon juice

1 tablespoon Dijon mustard

1 teaspoon minced fresh flat-leaf parsley

$1/2$ teaspoon dried basil

$1/2$ teaspoon dried oregano

$1/2$ teaspoon pepper, or to taste

TIP

Check the expiration date when buying yogurt; it will keep in a tightly closed container in the refrigerator. The watery layer in yogurt cartons is the whey rising to the top; stir it back in. It has nothing to do with the age or quality of the yogurt.

Process the cottage cheese, yogurt, oil, onion, garlic, lemon juice, and mustard in a blender until smooth and creamy. Stir in the remaining ingredients. Adjust the seasoning to taste.

PER TABLESPOON: Cal 25/Prot 1g/Carb 1.2g/Fat 1.8g/Chol 0mg/Sod 27mg

ADVANCE PREPARATION   This dressing will keep for up to 2 days in a tightly closed container in the refrigerator.

spinach and
strawberry salad
with pepper vinaigrette

Makes 4 servings

This is one of the most attractive salads I make. In fact, in my opinion, it warrants the purchase of a deep, clear glass salad bowl to do it justice!

3 cups torn stemmed salad spinach leaves (see Tips)

12 strawberries, halved

Pepper Vinaigrette

2 tablespoons canola or safflower oil	$^1/_4$ teaspoon pepper, or to taste
1 tablespoon cider vinegar	Dash of hot pepper sauce, or to taste
2 teaspoons honey	Dash of cayenne pepper, or to taste

GARNISH (OPTIONAL)   toasted sesame seeds

1. Toss the spinach with the strawberries in a large bowl.

2. Whisk together all of the dressing ingredients in a small bowl. Adjust the seasonings to taste. Add to the salad and toss again.

PER SERVING: Cal 96/Prot 1.5g/Carb 6.4g/Fat 7.1g/Chol 0mg/Sod 34mg

ADVANCE PREPARATION   This vinaigrette will keep for up to 2 weeks in a tightly closed container in the refrigerator. Toss the salad just before serving.

Variation

- Add $^1/_4$ cup toasted slivered almonds when tossing the salad.

TIPS

- Salad spinach, sold in most supermarkets, is tender, young, delicately flavored spinach leaves that have been pre-washed before packaging and are ready to use.

- To quickly remove a spinach stem, fold the leaf in half, pull and zip off the stem.

winter fruit
with curried
yogurt dressing

Makes 4 servings

This vibrant mixture of flavors and textures goes well with tomato-based soups, such as Winter Carrot Soup (page 50).

5 cups torn stemmed salad spinach leaves

1 apple, cut into $1/2$-inch cubes

1 pear, cut into $1/2$-inch cubes

1 rib celery, coarsely chopped

1 cup seedless green grapes

Curried Yogurt Dressing

$1/3$ cup nonfat plain yogurt

2 tablespoons fresh lemon juice

1 tablespoon honey

$1/2$ teaspoon curry powder, or to taste

Dash of ground cinnamon

GARNISH (OPTIONAL)   toasted sesame seeds, raw sunflower seeds, toasted coarsely chopped walnuts (see Tips)

1. Toss together the salad ingredients in a large bowl.

2. Stir together the dressing ingredients in a small bowl. Adjust the seasoning to taste. Add to the salad and toss.

PER SERVING: Cal 115/Prot 3.5g/Carb 24/Fat .6g/Chol 0mg/Sod 94mg

ADVANCE PREPARATION   This dressing will keep for 2 days in a tightly closed container in the refrigerator. Toss the salad just before serving.

Variations

- Substitute lettuce for spinach leaves.

- Substitute mayonnaise for part or all of the yogurt in the dressing.

> **TIPS**
>
> - Because of their high fat content, nuts quickly become rancid at room temperature. Refrigerate shelled nuts in an airtight container for up to 4 months; or freeze them for up to 6 months.
>
> - Toasting enhances the flavor and texture of most nuts. To toast nuts on the stovetop, stir or toss them in a dry skillet over medium-high heat for about 4 to 5 minutes or until they are golden brown. Immediately remove them from the skillet.

Rice and Spinach Salad with Asian Vinaigrette

rice and **spinach salad**
with **asian** vinaigrette

Makes 6 servings

Salads are one of the best ways to use leftover grains. Brown rice is my favorite for this salad, but wild rice or other grains, such as bulgur wheat or couscous, also work well. For a light summer supper or luncheon, serve this salad with soup, such as the Asian Stew (page 42), muffins, and a fruit dessert.

1¹/₂ cups cooked rice, preferably long-grain brown

4 cups coarsely shredded stemmed salad spinach leaves or arugula leaves (see Tip)

2 medium scallions, coarsely chopped

1 (11-ounce) can mandarin orange segments, drained

1 (8-ounce) can sliced water chestnuts, drained

¹/₂ cup toasted pine nuts or slivered almonds

Asian Vinaigrette

2 tablespoons canola or safflower oil

2 tablespoons white rice vinegar

2 tablespoons low-sodium soy sauce

¹/₂ teaspoon pepper, or to taste

¹/₂ teaspoon minced garlic

¹/₂ teaspoon minced fresh ginger

GARNISH (OPTIONAL)   blanched stemmed snow peas, currants or raisins

1. Toss together the salad ingredients in a large bowl.

(continues)

2. Whisk together the vinaigrette ingredients in a small bowl. Adjust the seasoning to taste. Add to the salad and toss.

PER SERVING: Cal 211/Prot 4.7g/Carb 23.2g/Fat 11.3g/Chol 0mg/Sod 229mg

ADVANCE PREPARATION   The salad can be covered and refrigerated for up to 4 hours before serving. To keep longer, it's best to refrigerate the dressing and salad in separate containers for up to 2 days, then combine the salad and dressing before serving.

> **TIP**
>
> Arugula, also called roquette or rocket, has long, spear-shaped leaves that resemble dandelion greens; they have a spicy, peppery, mustard-like bitterness and aroma. Select dark green leaves 3 to 5 inches long; the more mature the green, the stronger the flavor.

Variations

*   Substitute $1/2$ cup halved seedless red or green grapes for the mandarin orange segments.

*   Omit the mandarin oranges. Quickly sauté the sections from 1 orange in 1 tablespoon margarine with 1 tablespoon sugar added. Chill and cut into 1-inch pieces; toss into the salad.

*   To add hotness, add a few drops of hot pepper sauce or a dash of red pepper flakes to the dressing.

*   Substitute Chutney Dressing (page 75) for the Asian Vinaigrette.

indonesian
vegetable
salad

Makes 6 servings

*Thanks to the peanut butter and generous use of vegetables, this is a
filling dish that makes a surprising entrée salad.*

1 cup firm tofu cut into $1/2$-inch cubes

1 cup broccoli florets (see Tip)

1 cup cauliflower florets

2 plum tomatoes, cut into thin wedges

2 carrots, coarsely shredded

2 ribs celery, cut into julienne
strips

$1/2$ cucumber, thinly sliced

$1/2$ cup Szechuan Peanut Dressing
(page 126)

> **TIP**
>
> When buying broccoli, look for tight, dark
> green heads on firm but pliable stalks;
> slender stalks will be more tender. Many
> markets also sell florets separately. Store
> unwashed broccoli in an open plastic bag
> in the crisper drawer of your refrigerator; it
> will keep for up to 4 days.

GARNISH (OPTIONAL)   raisins, unsalted peanuts, toasted sesame seeds

Gently toss together the salad ingredients in a large bowl. Add the dressing and toss again.

PER SERVING: Cal 99/Prot 5.1g/Carb 8.7g/Fat 4.9g/Chol 0mg/Sod 112mg

ADVANCE PREPARATION   The salad ingredients and dressing can be prepared up to 4 hours in advance;
cover and refrigerate. Toss the salad with the dressing just before serving.

Variations

- Substitute other vegetables (up to 6 cups total). Try steamed green beans, fresh spinach leaves,
  blanched stemmed snow peas, sliced mushrooms, diced jicama, or slices of boiled new potatoes.

- Add Egg Threads (page 43; Tips) or slices of hard-cooked eggs.

- Spread the salad over a bed of cooked cellophane noodles; substitute Sesame-Soy Dressing
  (page 70) for the Szechuan Peanut Dressing.

85

thai
cucumber
salad

Makes 6 servings

Plan ahead to allow time for this sweet-sour salad to chill before serving. Serve it to accompany a spicy main course, such as the Vegetable Curry (page 138).

¹/₄ cup white rice vinegar

¹/₄ cup sugar

1 large cucumber, very thinly sliced (see Tips)

1 small shallot, very thinly sliced (see Tips)

1 tablespoon finely chopped and seeded hot red chile pepper

GARNISH (OPTIONAL)   sprigs of fresh cilantro or thinly sliced radishes

1. Stir together the vinegar and sugar in a small saucepan. Bring the mixture to a boil over medium-high heat, stirring occasionally, just until the sugar dissolves. Remove from the heat and allow to cool.

2. Toss together the remaining salad ingredients in a medium bowl. Add the vinegar mixture and toss again. Refrigerate until the salad is chilled. Use a slotted spoon for serving to strain the salad.

PER SERVING: Cal 43/Prot .5g/Carb 10g/Fat .1g/Chol 0mg/Sod 2mg

ADVANCE PREPARATION   This salad will keep for up to 2 days in a covered container in the refrigerator.

Variations

- When tossing the salad, add 1 very thinly sliced carrot.

- For a milder flavor, substitute a green chile pepper or jalapeño for the hot red chile pepper.

TIPS

- Many cucumbers are sold with a waxy coating to prolong their shelf life; the only way to remove the wax is by peeling. Better yet, buy unwaxed cucumbers. The elongated European cucumbers (sometimes called hothouse or English cucumbers) are the best choice. They have a mild flavor, more tender texture, and fewer seeds. Store whole cucumbers, unwashed, in a plastic bag in the refrigerator for up to 10 days; once cut, seal in plastic wrap and refrigerate for up to 5 days.

- Shallots, a member of the onion family, are small bulbous herbs with a mild onion-garlic flavor. Always use fresh shallots; dehydrated or powdered products will not do. (If unavailable, substitute some fresh onion and garlic.) Fresh shallots will keep for 1 month in the bottom bin of your refrigerator; use before they begin to sprout. When cooking, don't allow shallots to brown or they will taste bitter.

teriyaki
salad

Makes 6 servings

This salad travels well, great for a picnic or lunch-on-the-go. For variety, substitute other beans for the garbanzo beans, such as kidney beans or sweet beans (immature soy beans sold in the freezer section of most supermarkets).

1 (15-ounce) can garbanzo beans, drained and rinsed (1^3/$_4$ cups)

1^1/$_2$ cups sliced mushrooms

1 tomato, cut into ^{1}/$_2$-inch cubes

1 medium scallion, coarsely chopped

^{1}/$_2$ green bell pepper, coarsely chopped

^{1}/$_4$ cup minced fresh flat-leaf parsley (see Tip)

8 ounces firm tofu, cut into ^{1}/$_2$-inch cubes

Teriyaki Dressing

2 tablespoons white rice vinegar

2 tablespoons canola or safflower oil

1 tablespoon Dijon mustard

1 teaspoon low-sodium soy sauce

^{1}/$_2$ teaspoon minced garlic

^{1}/$_2$ teaspoon minced fresh ginger

^{1}/$_4$ teaspoon pepper, or to taste

2 tablespoons sesame seeds, preferably toasted

GARNISH (OPTIONAL)   red bell pepper strips

1. Toss together the salad ingredients, except the tofu, in a large bowl. Add the tofu and toss again.

2. Whisk together the dressing ingredients in a small bowl. Adjust the seasoning to taste. Add to the salad and toss.

PER SERVING: Cal 228/Prot 10g/Carb 24.7g/Fat 9.3g/Chol 0mg/Sod 71mg

ADVANCE PREPARATION   This salad will keep for up to 4 days in a covered container in the refrigerator.

TIP

To mince parsley very finely, dry it well with a paper towel or dish towel after washing it under cool running water. Damp parsley sticks together in clumps and will not separate after mincing it with a knife or in a food processor.

asian potato salad
with **soy** dressing

Makes 6 servings

This is not an authentic Asian dish, but the combination of flavors and textures is intriguing.

1 tablespoon honey

1½ pounds new potatoes (about 12), cut into 1-inch cubes or ½-inch-thick slices (see Tip)

1 cup sliced mushrooms

1 rib celery, diced

1 medium scallion, coarsely chopped

¼ cup minced fresh flat-leaf parsley

Soy Dressing

2 tablespoons canola or safflower oil

2 tablespoons white rice vinegar

1 tablespoon low-sodium soy sauce

1 tablespoon water

½ teaspoon minced garlic

½ teaspoon minced fresh ginger

GARNISH (OPTIONAL)   toasted sesame seeds, sprigs of fresh watercress or cilantro

1. Bring a medium pot of water to a boil over high heat. Stir in the honey; add the potatoes. When the water returns to a boil, reduce the heat to medium; cover and cook for about 8 minutes or until the potatoes are just tender.

2. While the potatoes are cooking, prepare the other salad ingredients. Whisk together the dressing ingredients in a small bowl.

3. When the potatoes are done, drain well. Transfer them to a large bowl; add the other salad ingredients and toss. Add the dressing and toss again. Bring the salad to room temperature for serving.

PER SERVING: Cal 118/Prot 1.7g/Carb 17.4g/Fat 4.6g/Chol 0mg/Sod 349mg

ADVANCE PREPARATION   To serve warm, serve this salad immediately after preparing. To serve chilled, it's best to refrigerate the dressing and salad in separate covered containers for up to 3 days; toss together up to 1 hour before serving.

TIP

Red new potatoes are young potatoes that are harvested before maturity. They are small, thin-skinned, low in starch, and sweet; and they are preferable for potato salads because mature baking potatoes break apart easily and absorb too much of the dressing. Do not refrigerate; instead, store new potatoes for up to 2 weeks at room temperature in a cool, dark place.

french potato salad
with savory
vinaigrette

Makes 6 servings

This potato salad does not contain mayonnaise; instead, the potatoes are tossed with an herb-seasoned vinaigrette. It's not the potato salad that Mom used to make.

1 bay leaf

2 tablespoons finely chopped onion

1/2 teaspoon pepper

1 1/2 pounds new potatoes (about 12), cut into 1-inch cubes or 1/2-inch-thick slices (see Tip)

Savory Vinaigrette

2 tablespoons extra-virgin olive oil

2 tablespoons white wine vinegar

1 tablespoon minced fresh flat-leaf parsley

1/2 teaspoon minced garlic

1 teaspoon dried summer savory

1/2 teaspoon pepper, or to taste

1/4 teaspoon powdered mustard

GARNISH (OPTIONAL)   halved cherry tomatoes, shredded Cheddar cheese mixed with minced fresh flat-leaf parsley

1. Bring a medium pot of water to a boil over high heat. Stir in the bay leaf, onion, and pepper; add the potatoes. When the water returns to a boil, reduce the heat to medium; cover and cook for about 8 minutes or until the potatoes are just tender.

2. While the potatoes are cooking, whisk together all of the dressing ingredients in a small bowl. Adjust the seasoning to taste.

3. When the potatoes are done; drain well and remove the bay leaf. Transfer the potatoes to a large bowl; add the dressing and toss. Bring the salad to room temperature for serving.

PER SERVING: Cal 98/Prot 1g/Carb 13.3g/Fat 4.5g/Chol 0mg/Sod 239mg

ADVANCE PREPARATION   To serve warm, serve this salad immediately after preparing. To serve chilled, it's best to refrigerate the dressing and salad in separate covered containers for up to 3 days; toss together up to 1 hour before serving.

Variation

- When tossing the salad, add other vegetables (up to 1 cup total). Try coarsely shredded carrots or steamed cut green beans.

TIP

It is not necessary to peel potatoes for potato salad; potatoes eaten with their skins have more nutrients. Scrub them well before cooking; many potatoes are sprayed with chemicals to keep their "eyes" from sprouting.

potato salad
with light
pesto vinaigrette

Makes 6 servings

If you love pesto, you'll love the flavor and aroma it adds to this potato salad. The Light Pesto Vinaigrette is also delicious as a sauce for sliced tomatoes, steamed asparagus, or steamed green beans, or as a dressing on green salads.

1 tablespoon honey

1^1/$_2$ pounds new potatoes (about 12), cut into 1-inch cubes or ^{1}/$_2$-inch-thick slices

1 carrot, coarsely shredded

^{1}/$_2$ green bell pepper, coarsely chopped

1 medium scallion, coarsely chopped

Light Pesto Vinaigrette

3 tablespoons white rice vinegar

2 tablespoons Basil Pesto (page 16)

2 tablespoons extra-virgin olive oil

1 tablespoon water

Dash of pepper, or to taste

GARNISH (OPTIONAL) freshly grated Parmesan cheese (see Tip)

1. Bring a medium pot of water to a boil over high heat. Stir in the honey; add the potatoes. When the water returns to a boil, reduce the heat to medium; cover and cook for about 8 minutes or until the potatoes are just tender.

2. Process all of the dressing ingredients in a food processor until smooth. Adjust the seasoning to taste.

3. When the potatoes are done, drain well. Transfer them to a large bowl; add the other salad ingredients and toss. Add the dressing and toss again. Serve warm or bring the salad to room temperature.

PER SERVING: Cal 134/Prot 1.6g/Carb 16.8g/Fat 6.7g/Chol 0mg/Sod 248mg

ADVANCE PREPARATION   To serve warm, serve this salad immediately after preparing. To serve chilled, it's best to refrigerate the dressing and salad in separate covered containers for up to 3 days; toss together up to 1 hour before serving.

TIP

Always buy freshly grated Parmesan cheese or use a hand grater or food processor to grate your own from a block of Parmesan. Commercially packaged, grated Parmesan cheese, which is sold unrefrigerated, is loaded with preservatives and is overly salty.

couscous-currant salad
with **lemon** dressing

Makes 4 servings

Couscous makes this refreshing salad very quick to prepare. For variety, add beans and other vegetables such as shredded carrots or finely chopped red bell pepper.

1 cup vegetable stock (see page xxiv and 3) or water

1 cup couscous

Lemon Dressing

$^1/_4$ cup fresh lemon juice

2 tablespoons extra-virgin olive oil

$^1/_4$ teaspoon ground cinnamon

$^1/_4$ teaspoon pepper, or to taste

$^1/_4$ teaspoon turmeric

Few drops of hot pepper sauce, or to taste

To Complete the Recipe

$^1/_3$ cup currants (see Tip)

$^1/_4$ cup toasted pine nuts

1 rib celery, diced

1 medium scallion, finely chopped

2 tablespoons minced fresh flat-leaf parsley

GARNISH (OPTIONAL)   asparagus tips or minced fresh chives

1. Heat the stock or water, until hot but not boiling, in a small saucepan over medium-high heat. Remove the pan from the heat; stir in the couscous. Let stand, covered, for about 5 to 10 minutes or until the liquid is completely absorbed.

2. Meanwhile, whisk together the dressing ingredients in a small bowl. Adjust the seasonings to taste.

3. When couscous has softened, toss with a fork. Add the remaining ingredients and toss. Add the dressing and toss again.

ADVANCE PREPARATION   This salad will keep well for up to 4 days in a covered container in the refrigerator. For storage longer than 1 day, add the dressing just before serving because it is absorbed as the salad stands.

Variations

* In the Lemon Dressing, substitute 1 to 2 teaspoons curry powder (to taste) for the ground cinnamon and turmeric.

* Substitute $1/3$ cup Chutney Dressing (page 75) for the Lemon Dressing.

> **TIP**
>
> Currants are about $1/4$ the size of raisins; they are less sweet but have a stronger flavor. They are found in the supermarket with the dried fruits.

*Pasta Salad Primavera with
Herbed Tomato Sauce (page 76)*

pasta salad **primavera**

Makes 8 servings

The goodness of pasta, crisp-tender vegetables, and cheese combine with your choice of dressing in this salad. This is my personal favorite pasta salad; I've served it at a buffet for fifty and often keep it in the refrigerator for weekend lunches and snacks.

8 ounces corkscrew pasta (rotini or
  rotelle); (see Tips)

2 cups broccoli florets

1 cup Herbed Tomato Sauce (page 76)

To Complete the Recipe

1 cup mozzarella cheese cut into
  $1/2$-inch cubes

1 small zucchini, cut into $1/2$-inch cubes

1 red bell pepper, coarsely chopped

1 cup frozen peas (preferably baby peas),
  thawed

1 plum tomato, cut into $1/2$-inch cubes
  (see Tips)

2 medium scallions, coarsely chopped

GARNISH (OPTIONAL)   freshly grated Parmesan cheese, freshly ground black pepper, sprigs of fresh basil, toasted pine nuts

1. Bring a large pot of water to a boil; add the pasta. When the water returns to a boil, stir occasionally to separate the pasta. Reduce the heat to medium-high and cook for about 8 to 10 minutes, or according to package instructions, until the pasta is *al dente*.

2. While the pasta is cooking, put the broccoli into a small microwave-proof dish; add about $1/4$ cup water. Cover and microwave on high for about 4 minutes or until

crisp-tender. (Or cook the broccoli for about 4 minutes in a stovetop steamer.) Drain and rinse well in cold water, then drain again.

3. Meanwhile, prepare the Herbed Tomato Sauce.

4. When the pasta is done, drain and rinse well in cold water, then drain again.

5. Transfer the pasta to a large bowl. Add the broccoli and the remaining salad ingredients; toss. Add the dressing and toss again.

PER SERVING: Cal 121/Prot 7.6g/Carb 16.8g/Fat 2.6g/Chol 8mg/Sod 171mg

ADVANCE PREPARATION   This salad will keep for up to 3 days in a covered container in the refrigerator. It's best to refrigerate the dressing and salad separately; toss together up to 1 hour before serving.

TIPS

- Rotini is a small corkscrew-shaped pasta; rotelle is the same shape but larger.

- Plum tomatoes, often called Italian or Roma tomatoes, have thick, meaty walls, little juice, and a rich, sweet flavor. They are the best choice for recipes that benefit from less juicy tomatoes or those that retain their shape after being chopped or sliced.

Variations

- Substitute or add other vegetables (up to 8 cups total). Try steamed carrot slices or cut asparagus.

- For the Herbed Tomato Sauce, substitute any of the following: 1 cup Yogurt-Parmesan Dressing (page 77), 1 cup Creamy Italian Dressing (page 78), $1/2$ cup Honey-Poppyseed Dressing (page 69), $1/2$ cup Tangy Honey-Mustard Dressing (page 71), $1/2$ cup Basic Vinaigrette (page 72), or $1/2$ cup Light Pesto Vinaigrette (page 94). (The thinner dressings require less to moisten the salad.)

- Omit the cheese; substitute 1 cup cooked beans, such as cannellini beans (Italian white kidney beans).

basil-bean salad

Makes 6 servings

This crunchy, colorful salad is perfect for those occasions, like picnics, when you need a salad that can be prepared ahead and will not wilt or spoil. For dining at home, serve it as an accompaniment to the Guacamole Omelet with Tomato Hot Sauce (page 156).

1 (15-ounce) can Great Northern beans, drained and rinsed (1^3/$_4$ cups)

1 cucumber, coarsely chopped

1 red bell pepper, coarsely chopped (see Tip)

^{1}/$_4$ cup finely chopped red onion

Dressing

2 tablespoons canola or safflower oil

2 tablespoons cider vinegar

1 tablespoon fresh lemon juice

2 tablespoons minced fresh basil (or 2 teaspoons dried basil)

1 tablespoon minced fresh flat-leaf parsley

^{1}/$_4$ teaspoon pepper, or to taste

GARNISH (OPTIONAL)   coarsely chopped scallions

1. Toss together the salad ingredients in a medium bowl.

2. Whisk together the dressing ingredients in a small bowl. Adjust the seasoning to taste. Add to the bean mixture and toss. Strain the salad with a slotted spoon for serving.

PER SERVING: Cal 153/Prot 6.9g/Carb 20.1g/Fat 5g/Chol 0mg/Sod 4mg

> ### TIP
>
> Bell peppers are most often sold in the mature green stage, fully developed but not yet ripe. Red bell peppers are vine-ripened green peppers; they are sweeter because of the longer ripening. Store bell peppers for up to 1 week in plastic bags in the refrigerator.

ADVANCE PREPARATION   This salad will keep for up to 4 days in a covered container in the refrigerator.

pasta-asparagus
salad

Makes 4 servings

For a summer grilled flavor, rather than steaming the asparagus cook them on an outdoor grill or stovetop grill pan (see page xxx).

8 ounces penne (see Tips)

3 cups asparagus diagonally cut into
 3-inch-long pieces (see Tips)

1 cup Creamy Italian Dressing (page 78)

To Complete the Recipe

1 cup halved cherry tomatoes

1 red bell pepper, coarsely chopped

2 carrots, coarsely shredded

GARNISH (OPTIONAL)   minced chives, sprigs of fresh basil or flat-leaf parsley

1. Bring a large pot of water to a boil; add the penne. When the water returns to a boil, stir occasionally to separate the pasta. Reduce the heat to medium-high and cook for about 12 to 14 minutes, or according to package instructions, until the pasta is *al dente*.

2. While the penne is cooking, put the asparagus into a medium microwave-proof dish; add about 1/4 cup water. Cover and microwave on high for about 4 minutes or until crisp-tender. (Or cook the asparagus for about 4 minutes in a stovetop steamer.) Drain and rinse well in cold water, then drain again.

3. Prepare the Creamy Italian Dressing.

4. When the pasta is done, drain and rinse well in cold water, then drain again.

5. Transfer the pasta to a large bowl. Add the asparagus and the remaining salad ingredients; toss. Add the dressing and toss again.

PER SERVING: Cal 266/Prot 8.2g/Carb 39.9g/Fat 8.2g/Chol 0mg/Sod 413mg

ADVANCE PREPARATION   This salad will keep for up to 3 days in a covered container in the refrigerator. It's best to refrigerate the dressing and salad separately; toss together up to 1 hour before serving.

Variation

- For the dressing, substitute any of the following: 1 cup Herbed Tomato Sauce (page 76), 1 cup Yogurt-Parmesan Dressing (page 77), $1/2$ cup Honey-Poppyseed Dressing (page 69), $1/2$ cup Tangy Honey-Mustard Dressing (page 71), $1/2$ cup Basic Vinaigrette (page 72), or $1/2$ cup Light Pesto Vinaigrette (page 94). (The thinner dressings require less to moisten the salad.)

TIPS

- Penne is diagonally cut, large straight tubes of macaroni.

- Asparagus is best in the early spring. Choose bright green spears with firm stalks; the tips should be tightly closed and have a lavender hue. Slender stalks are more tender. Thick stalks can be halved lengthwise or peeled.

- To store asparagus, wrap the stalks in a plastic bag and store in the vegetable crisper; use within 2 to 3 days. If wilted, stand the stalks in a jar filled with 2 inches of very cold water. Cover with a plastic bag, seal, and refrigerate for 1 to 2 hours before cooking.

szechuan pasta salad
with hot pepper
vinaigrette

Makes 4 servings

Adjust the amount of hot pepper sauce and cayenne pepper in the dressing for this Asian pasta salad to make it mild or fiery.

8 ounces bow tie pasta (farfalle)

3 cups broccoli florets

1$^1/_2$ cups stemmed snow peas (about 4 ounces)

Hot Pepper Vinaigrette

$^1/_3$ cup canola or safflower oil

$^1/_3$ cup red wine vinegar

2 tablespoons honey

$^1/_2$ teaspoon minced garlic

2 tablespoons sesame seeds, preferably toasted

2 teaspoons hot pepper sauce, or to taste

1 teaspoon minced fresh ginger

Pinch of cayenne pepper, or to taste

To Complete the Recipe

1 red bell pepper, cut into thin strips

3 medium scallions, cut into $^1/_2$-inch-long pieces

GARNISH (OPTIONAL)   toasted pine nuts

1. Bring a large pot of water to a boil; add the bow ties. When the water returns to a boil, stir occasionally to separate the pasta. Reduce the heat to medium-high and cook for about 12 to 14 minutes, or according to package instructions, until the pasta is *al dente*.

2. While the pasta is cooking, blanch the broccoli and snow peas. Also, whisk together the vinaigrette ingredients in a small bowl.

3. When the pasta is done, drain and rinse well in cold water, then drain again.

4. Transfer the pasta to a large bowl. Add the broccoli, snow peas, bell pepper, and scallions; toss. Add the vinaigrette and toss again. Adjust the seasoning to taste.

PER SERVING: Cal 385/Prot 9.2g/Carb 40.7g/Fat 20.6g/Chol 0mg/Sod 50mg

ADVANCE PREPARATION   This salad will keep for up to 3 days in a covered container in the refrigerator. It's best to refrigerate the dressing and salad separately; toss together up to 1 hour before serving.

chapter 4 *Salads*

TIP

When cooking pasta for a spicy dish, add about 1 teaspoon hot pepper sauce to the cooking water to infuse the pasta with a subtle pepper flavor.

thai
noodle
salad

Makes 6 servings

My friend from Thailand shared this authentic, spicy recipe with me. It's one of my favorites and always makes a big hit with guests.

8 ounces cellophane noodles (see Tip)

1 cup unsalted, dry-roasted peanuts

$1/4$ cup minced fresh ginger or a peeled piece of fresh ginger about 1-inch-thick and 4 inches long

1 hot red chili pepper (seeds removed), or to taste

$1/4$ cup finely chopped fresh basil, mint, or cilantro

$1/2$ cup fresh lime juice

$1/4$ cup low-sodium soy sauce

$1/4$ cup sugar

GARNISH (OPTIONAL)   finely chopped unsalted, dry-roasted peanuts, red bell pepper rings

1. Bring a medium pot of water to boil over high heat; remove from the heat. Add the noodles; soak, stirring occasionally, for about 8 to 10 minutes, or according to package instructions, until the noodles are softened and clear. (If the noodles are thick, it may be necessary to cook them in boiling water.)

2. While the noodles are soaking, combine the peanuts, ginger, and chili pepper in a food processor or electric mincer. Process until the ginger is finely chopped and the peanuts are slightly chunky.

3. When the noodles are softened and clear, drain and rinse well in cold water, then drain again.

4. Transfer the noodles to a large bowl; use kitchen shears to cut them into about 6-inch lengths. Add the ginger mixture and toss. Add the basil, mint, or cilantro and toss again.

5. Combine the remaining ingredients in a measuring cup; stir until sugar is dissolved. Pour over the salad and toss until the lime juice mixture is evenly distributed.

PER SERVING: Cal 338/Prot 6.8g/Carb 50.2g/Fat 12.2g/Chol 0mg/Sod 407mg

ADVANCE PREPARATION   This salad can be covered and refrigerated for up to 8 hours; let stand at room temperature for about $1/2$ hour before serving.

Variations

• For a milder flavor, substitute green chili pepper or jalapeño pepper for the hot red chili pepper, or use less hot red chili pepper. For a hotter flavor, leave in the chili pepper seeds, or add more chili pepper.

• Substitute about $1/2$ teaspoon red pepper flakes for the fresh chili pepper.

> ### TIP
>
> Cellophane noodles, also called bean thread noodles, glass noodles, or sai fun, are made with the starch of mung beans, which we know best as bean sprouts. They are brittle and have a cellophane-like translucence. Purchase them in Asian markets and in some supermarkets. They will keep indefinitely when stored in an airtight container.

pasta and couscous salad
with spicy
peanut dressing

Makes 6 servings

This colorful salad is a favorite among students in my pasta cooking classes. If you prefer, substitute cooked beans, such as garbanzo beans, for the peanuts.

6 ounces spinach ribbon noodles (about 3¹/₂ cups uncooked)

¹/₂ cup vegetable stock (see pages xxiv and 3) or water

¹/₂ cup couscous

Spicy Peanut Dressing

¹/₄ cup white rice vinegar

3 tablespoons extra-virgin olive oil

3 tablespoons smooth peanut butter

1 tablespoon honey

¹/₂ teaspoon minced garlic

¹/₄ teaspoon cayenne pepper, or to taste (see Tip)

Water, as needed

To Complete the Recipe

1 red bell pepper, coarsely chopped

¹/₂ cup unsalted, dry-roasted peanuts

2 medium scallions, thinly sliced

¹/₄ cup minced fresh flat-leaf parsley

GARNISH (OPTIONAL)   mandarin orange segments or pineapple chunks, raisins

1. Bring a large pot of water to a boil over high heat; add the noodles. When the water returns to a boil, stir occasionally to separate the noodles. Reduce the heat to medium-high and cook for about 5 to 7 minutes, or according to package instructions, until the noodles are *al dente*.

2. Heat the stock or water, until hot but not boiling, in a small saucepan over medium-high heat. Remove the pan from the heat; stir in the couscous. Let stand, covered, for about 5 to 10 minutes or until the liquid is completely absorbed.

3. Meanwhile, whisk together the dressing ingredients, except the water. The dressing should have a cake-batter consistency; add water as needed.

4. When the noodles are done, drain well and rinse under cold water; then drain again. Fluff the couscous with a fork.

5. Toss together the bell pepper, peanuts, scallions, and parsley in a large bowl. Add the noodles and couscous; toss. Add the dressing and toss again. Adjust the seasoning to taste.

PER SERVING: Cal 264/Prot 7.3g/Carb 19.5g/Fat 17.4g/Chol 9mg/Sod 10mg

ADVANCE PREPARATION   Toss the salad ingredients and make the dressing up to 1 day in advance; cover and refrigerate separately. Toss the salad with the dressing just before serving.

Variation

- Substitute bulgur wheat (see page 6) or quinoa (see page 6) for the couscous.

> **TIP**
>
> Cayenne is the ground dried pod of the small, more pungent varieties of chile peppers. Use with caution, because it is very hot. Store cayenne in a tightly closed container in the refrigerator to retain its color and flavor.

chapter 5

Entrées

IF YOU HAVE ONLY 15 MINUTES, MOST OF THE RECIPES

in this chapter will stand on their own, with the addition

of a simple salad. Most of the dishes include a protein

source; and you'll find a wide variety of vegetables,

legumes, nuts, cheeses, and seasonings.

Pasta and rice are classic vegetarian partners to meatless accompaniments because of their beguilingly neutral, substantial qualities. When paired with protein, these complex carbohydrates become a satisfying, nutritious meal. You'll also find a few egg dishes here. We eat them sparingly, about once a week; and these are some of my favorites. If you prefer, you can substitute cholesterol-free egg substitute, which I often use, too. Many of the entrées are inspired by dishes from other cultures (India, China, Italy); all are bold and flavorful.

These recipes are simple enough to make for your family on busy weekdays, yet many are "gourmet" enough to please your discriminating guests.

pasta marinara
on **beds** of
spinach

Makes 4 servings

You can make the Marinara Sauce in advance, but toss it with hot, freshly cooked pasta just before serving. If you'd like, add steamed chopped vegetables to add texture to the sauce, before tossing it with the penne or pasta of your choice.

2 cups Marinara Sauce (page 19)

8 ounces penne rigate (see Tips)

1 (10-ounce) package frozen chopped spinach

2 tablespoons fresh lemon juice

Dash of pepper, or to taste

GARNISH (OPTIONAL)   freshly grated Parmesan cheese, freshly ground black pepper (see Tips), toasted pine nuts

1. Bring a large pot of water to a boil over high heat.

2. Prepare or reheat the Marinara Sauce.

3. When the water comes to a boil, add the penne. When the water returns to a boil, stir occasionally to separate the penne. Reduce the heat to medium-high and cook for about 12 to 14 minutes, or according to package instructions, until the pasta is *al dente*.

4. Meanwhile, cook the spinach according to package instructions; drain well.

5. When the penne is done, drain well.

6. To serve, spread a layer of spinach on each dinner plate. Drizzle with lemon juice and sprinkle with pepper. Add a layer of pasta and top with the Marinara Sauce.

> ## TIPS
>
> - The fluted surface of penne "rigate" helps the sauce to adhere to the noodles.
>
> - Freshly ground or cracked whole dried peppercorns are more flavorful than pre-ground pepper because, once cracked, the peppercorn immediately releases much of its oil as aroma and flavor. The best pepper grinders have settings for both coarse and fine grinds. Store whole peppercorns in a cool, dark place for up to 1 year.

PER SERVING: Cal 225/Prot 8g/Carb 38.6g/Fat 4.3g/Chol 0mg/Sod 497mg

Variation

- Substitute cooked rice for the pasta.

pasta with **shells** lemon vinaigrette

Makes 4 servings

With a little advance planning, this can be the refreshing entrée for dinner on a steamy summer night. As an accompaniment, serve crusty French bread with Pesto Herb Spread (page 17) and Maple Oranges Amandine (page 165) for dessert.

12 jumbo pasta shells

1$^{1}/_{2}$ cups nonfat ricotta cheese

$^{1}/_{2}$ cup finely chopped almonds

3 tablespoons snipped fresh chives

2 tablespoons lemon zest (see Tip)

$^{3}/_{4}$ teaspoon pepper

Lemon Vinaigrette

$^{1}/_{4}$ cup fresh lemon juice

2 tablespoons extra-virgin olive oil

1 teaspoon Dijon mustard

2 tablespoons minced fresh flat-leaf
   parsley

1 tablespoon minced fresh basil
   (or 1 teaspoon dried basil)

$^{1}/_{2}$ teaspoon minced garlic

GARNISH (OPTIONAL)   freshly grated Parmesan cheese, toasted sliced almonds or pine nuts, cherry tomatoes, sprigs of fresh basil

1. Bring a large pot of water to a boil over high heat; add the shells. When the water returns to a boil, stir occasionally to separate the shells. Reduce the heat to medium-high and cook for about 12 minutes, or according to package instructions, until the shells are tender.

2. While the pasta is cooking, combine the remaining stuffed shell ingredients in a medium bowl.

3. Whisk together the vinaigrette ingredients in a large bowl.

4. When the shells are done, drain well; rinse under cold water and drain well again (pat dry with paper towels, if necessary). Add the shells to the vinaigrette and toss. Remove with a slotted spoon, reserving the vinaigrette.

5. Stuff the shells with the ricotta cheese mixture, allowing about 1 heaping tablespoon for each. Arrange the stuffed shells on a serving platter; drizzle with the reserved vinaigrette.

PER SERVING: Cal 394/Prot 17.5g/Carb 35.1g/Fat 20.4g/Chol 14mg/Sod 99mg

ADVANCE PREPARATION   This dish can be assembled early in the day for an evening meal; cover and refrigerate.

Variations

- Substitute 6 pieces of lasagna for the pasta shells; spread each with some of the filling, then roll up jelly-roll fashion.

- Substitute $1/2$ to 1 cup mashed firm tofu for part of the ricotta cheese.

- Substitute Herbed Tomato Sauce (page 76) for the Lemon Vinaigrette. Follow the same procedure for tossing the shells with the dressing. Pour half of the remaining sauce on the serving platter, arrange shells, and top with the remaining sauce.

TIP

Zesting is done with a kitchen gadget called a zester, which has a short, flat blade with a beveled end and five small holes. When drawn firmly over the skin of a lemon, lime, or orange, the tool removes long, thin strips of the colored zest. If you do not have a zester, use a vegetable peeler; cut the peel into thin strips with a small knife. Before zesting citrus rind, scrub the fruit well, then dry it thoroughly. Remove only the outer, colored part; the white portion beneath tastes bitter.

Pasta al Pesto

pasta
al pesto

Makes 6 servings

This is a very versatile recipe. Vary the pasta, using either short cuts, such as penne, or long strands, like linguine. Substitute or add chopped tomatoes or nearly any vegetable. The pesto can be made in advance, but toss it with the hot pasta just after they are cooked.

> ### TIP
> Like other squashes, zucchini are 95 percent water, so cook them quickly or they will become mushy.

8 ounces pasta

2 tablespoons olive oil

1 small zucchini, thinly sliced (see Tip)

2 carrots, coarsely shredded

$1/4$ cup finely chopped red bell pepper

$1/2$ cup Basil Pesto (page 16)

GARNISH (OPTIONAL)   freshly ground black pepper, freshly grated Parmesan or Romano cheese

1. Bring a large pot of water to a boil over high heat; add the pasta. When the water returns to a boil, stir occasionally to separate the pasta. Reduce the heat to medium-high and cook according to package instructions, until the pasta is *al dente*.

2. While the pasta is cooking, heat the oil in a large nonstick skillet over medium-high heat. Add the zucchini, carrots, and bell pepper; cook, stirring occasionally, for about 5 minutes or until the vegetables are tender.

3. Meanwhile, make the pesto.

4. When the pasta is done, drain well; return to the pot. Add the pesto and toss. Add the cooked vegetables; toss again.

PER SERVING: Cal 231/Prot 5g/Carb 22.9/Fat 13.3g/Chol 0mg/Sod 32mg

pasta
with herbed ricotta
and pine nuts

Makes 4 servings

Serve this simple but elegant dish with crusty French bread and a spinach and mushroom salad tossed with Basic Vinaigrette (page 72) and garnished with Herbed Garlic Croutons (page 64).

8 ounces spinach noodles	2 tablespoons minced fresh flat-leaf parsley
2 tablespoons butter	1 teaspoon grated lemon rind
1/4 cup finely chopped onion	1/4 cup fresh lemon juice
1 teaspoon minced garlic	1/2 teaspoon dried tarragon
3/4 cup nonfat ricotta cheese	1/2 teaspoon pepper, or to taste
1/2 cup toasted pine nuts (see Tips)	

GARNISH (OPTIONAL)   halved cherry tomatoes, strips of red bell pepper, steamed asparagus spears, sprigs of fresh flat-leaf parsley, freshly grated Parmesan cheese

1. Bring a large pot of water to a boil over high heat; add the noodles. When the water returns to a boil, stir occasionally to separate the noodles. Reduce the heat to medium-high and cook for about 8 to 10 minutes, or according to package instructions, until the noodles are *al dente*.

2. While the pasta is cooking, melt the butter in a small nonstick skillet over medium-high heat. Add the onion, cook, stirring occasionally, for about 5 minutes or until the onion is softened. Reduce the heat to low.

3. Add the remaining ingredients to the skillet; heat, stirring occasionally just until warm.

4. When the noodles are done, drain well; return to the pot. Add the ricotta mixture and toss gently. Adjust the seasoning to taste.

PER SERVING: Cal 205/Prot 7.4g/Carb 23.8g/Fat 8.9g/Chol 23mg/Sod 112mg

ADVANCE PREPARATION   This sauce will keep for up to 2 days in a covered container in the refrigerator. Heat gently before tossing with hot, freshly cooked pasta.

Variation

• Substitute basil for the tarragon.

TIPS

• Pine nuts (also called pignoli nuts, pignolia, or pinons) are the seeds from the cone of certain pine trees. Their natural oil turns rancid very quickly, so store them in the refrigerator for up to 1 month or freeze for up to 3 months.

• The sweet, mild flavor of pine nuts is enhanced by toasting: Put them in a small skillet over medium heat; stir constantly for about 4 to 5 minutes or until the nuts are lightly browned. Immediately remove from the pan. I usually toast 1 cup at a time and freeze the nuts until I need them to garnish pasta dishes, soups, and salads.

pasta
with ricotta-walnut
sauce

Makes 4 servings

Always toss this sauce with hot, freshly cooked pasta. Serve immediately, while warm, or allow to cool.

8 ounces vermicelli

Ricotta-Walnut Sauce

$1/2$ cup nonfat ricotta cheese (see Tip)	1 teaspoon minced garlic
$1/2$ cup nonfat plain yogurt	$1/2$ cup minced fresh flat-leaf parsley
$1/2$ cup coarsely chopped walnuts	1 tablespoon minced fresh basil (or
$1/4$ cup freshly grated Parmesan cheese	1 teaspoon dried basil)
1 tablespoon butter, softened	$1/2$ teaspoon pepper, or to taste

GARNISH (OPTIONAL)   freshly ground black pepper, freshly grated Parmesan cheese, cherry tomatoes, broccoli florets

1. Bring a large pot of water to a boil over high heat; add the vermicelli. When the water returns to a boil, stir occasionally to separate the pasta. Reduce the heat to medium-high and cook for about 9 to 11 minutes, or according to package instructions, until the pasta is *al dente*.

2. While the pasta is cooking, process the ricotta cheese, yogurt, walnuts, Parmesan, butter, and garlic in a food processor until smooth. Stir in the remaining ingredients. Transfer to a small nonstick saucepan; heat, stirring occasionally, just until warm.

3. When the pasta is done, drain well. Return to the pot; add the sauce and toss. Adjust the seasoning to taste.

PER SERVING: Cal 294/Prot 13.1g/Carb 24.5g/Fat 15.9g/Chol 23mg/Sod 211mg

ADVANCE PREPARATION   This sauce will keep for up to 2 days in a covered container in the refrigerator. Heat gently over low heat before tossing with hot, freshly cooked pasta.

Variations

- When tossing the sauce with the pasta, add steamed vegetables (up to 2 cups total). Try peas, broccoli florets, or cut green beans.

- For fettucine almost-alfredo: Substitute $1/4$ cup milk and $1/4$ cup vegetable stock (see pages xxiv and 3) for the yogurt; omit the garlic, walnuts, parsley, and basil; garnish with almond slices, sprigs of fresh flat-leaf parsley, and cherry tomatoes or steamed cut asparagus.

> **TIP**
>
> Ricotta is made from the whey that remains after the production of such cheeses as provolone and mozzarella. The whey is blended with whole or skim milk; ricotta, therefore, is not a true cheese because it is not made from curd.

chickpea-zucchini
curry

Makes 4 servings

This vegetarian dish made with chickpeas (or garbanzos) is a treat for curry lovers. In place of the egg noodles, it can be served over spaghetti, rice, or couscous.

2 tablespoons canola or safflower oil

1 1/2 cups sliced mushrooms

1 small zucchini, halved lengthwise and
   cut into 1/4-inch-thick slices

1/4 cup coarsely chopped onion

1/2 teaspoon minced garlic

2 teaspoons curry powder

1 (15-ounce) can chickpeas, drained
   and rinsed (1 1/2 cups)

1 (6-ounce) can tomato paste

1 cup water

1 large tomato, cut into 1/2-inch cubes

1/4 teaspoon pepper, or to taste

8 ounces wide egg noodles

GARNISH (OPTIONAL)   scallion curls (see Tip)

1. Bring a large pot of water to a boil over high heat.

2. Heat the oil in a large nonstick sauté pan over medium-high heat. Add the mushrooms, zucchini, onion, garlic, and curry powder; cook, stirring occasionally, for about 5 minutes or until the zucchini is tender but not mushy. Add the remaining ingredients except noodles; cover and cook, stirring occasionally, over medium heat for about 6 minutes. Adjust the seasoning to taste.

3. While the sauce is cooking, add the noodles to the pot of boiling water. When the water returns to a boil, stir occasionally to separate the noodles. Reduce the heat to medium-high and cook for about 6 to 8 minutes, or according to package instructions, until the noodles are tender. When the noodles are done, drain well.

4. Spoon the vegetable mixture over individual servings of noodles.

PER SERVING: Cal 411/Prot 15.5g/Carb 61.1g/Fat 11.6g/Chol 0mg/Sod 417mg

TIP

To make scallion curls: Slice the green parts of scallions *very* thinly lengthwise. Drop into a bowl of ice water. Curls will form in about 10 to 15 minutes.

pasta
with **chinese**
tahini sauce

Makes 4 servings

This simple, uncooked sauce is abundant with the full-bodied flavors of tahini and chili paste with garlic. Adjust the amount of chili paste to suit your taste. It's fiery! Serve the dish warm, and enjoy the leftovers at room temperature the next day.

8 ounces thin buckwheat (soba) noodles (see Tips)

Chinese Tahini Sauce

2 tablespoons tahini

1 tablespoon white rice vinegar

1 tablespoon low-sodium soy sauce

1 tablespoon dark sesame oil

2 teaspoons chili paste with garlic, or to
taste (see Tips)

1 teaspoon minced fresh ginger

Dash of pepper, or to taste

Water, as needed

To Complete the Recipe

1 cup frozen peas (preferably baby peas), thawed

GARNISH (OPTIONAL)   toasted sesame seeds or chopped, unsalted dry-roasted peanuts, scallion curls (see Tip, page 123), sprigs of fresh cilantro

1. Bring a large pot of water to a boil over high heat; add the noodles. When the water returns to a boil, stir occasionally to separate the noodles. Reduce the heat to medium-high and cook for about 6 to 8 minutes, or according to package instructions, until the noodles are *al dente*.

2. While the noodles are cooking, whisk together the sauce ingredients in a small bowl. The sauce should have a cake-batter consistency; add water as needed.

3. When the noodles are done, drain well; return to the pot. Add the peas and toss. Add the sauce and toss again. Adjust the seasoning to taste.

PER SERVING: Cal 87/Prot 2.2g/Carb .8g/Fat 8.3g/Chol 0mg/Sod 151mg

ADVANCE PREPARATION   This sauce will keep for up to 1 week in a tightly closed container in the refrigerator. Bring to room temperature before tossing with hot, freshly cooked pasta. Even if you plan to serve this dish cold or at room temperature, toss the dressing with hot pasta, then chill. The completed dish will keep for up to 3 days in a covered container in the refrigerator.

Variation

- Add additional vegetables such as sautéed sliced mushrooms, steamed broccoli florets, steamed sliced carrots, blanched stemmed snow peas, minced red bell pepper, or finely chopped scallions; if you add several, the amount of dressing will need to be increased.

TIPS

- Soba noodles are Japanese noodles made from an ancient traditional recipe. Originally the brownish-gray noodles were made with buckwheat flour, water, and salt; today wheat flour is also added.

- Chili paste with garlic, also called chili purée or Chinese chili sauce, is found in Asian markets and in the Asian foods section of most supermarkets. Refrigerate it after opening.

pasta
with szechuan
peanut dressing

Makes 6 servings

If you like your food spicy, add more red pepper flakes to make this dish fiery!

8 ounces linguine

2 cups broccoli florets

Szechuan Peanut Dressing

$1/3$ cup peanut butter, smooth or chunky

$1/2$ cup hot vegetable stock (see pages xxiv and 3) or hot water, or as needed

1 teaspoon low-sodium soy sauce (see Tip)

2 tablespoons white rice vinegar

2 tablespoons canola or safflower oil

1 teaspoon minced garlic

$1/2$ teaspoon red pepper flakes, or to taste

To Complete the Recipe

2 cups cherry tomatoes

GARNISH (OPTIONAL)   minced scallions

1. Bring a large pot of water to a boil; add the linguine. When the water returns to a boil, stir occasionally to separate the linguine. Reduce the heat to medium-high and cook for about 10 to 12 minutes, or according to package instructions, until the pasta is *al dente*.

2. While the pasta is cooking, put the broccoli florets into a medium microwave-proof dish; add about $1/4$ cup water. Cover and microwave on high for about 4 minutes, or until crisp-tender. (Or cook the broccoli for about 4 minutes in a stovetop steamer.) Drain well.

3. Meanwhile, in a medium bowl, whisk together the peanut butter and $1/2$ cup of the stock or water until smooth. Stir in the remaining dressing ingredients. The sauce should have a cake-batter consistency; add more stock or water as needed.

4. When the linguine is done, drain well; return to the pot. Add the dressing and toss. Add the broccoli and tomatoes; toss again. Adjust the seasoning to taste.

PER SERVING: Cal 133/Prot 4.4g/Carb 15.9g/Fat 5.7g/Chol 0mg/Sod 53mg

ADVANCE PREPARATION   This dressing will keep for up to 1 week in a tightly closed container in the refrigerator. Bring to room temperature and toss with hot, freshly cooked pasta. Even if you plan to serve this dish cold or at room temperature, toss the dressing with hot pasta, then chill.

> **TIP**
>
> Low-sodium or "lite" soy sauce contains about 40 percent less sodium than traditional soy sauce or tamari, but it provides nearly the same flavor. Soy sauce will keep almost indefinitely in the refrigerator.

Variation

• Use the Szechuan Peanut Dressing as a warm topping for steamed vegetables, such as green beans, broccoli, or cauliflower.

triple
cheese-poppyseed
noodles

Makes 6 servings

This is a reduced-fat version of a recipe my mom used to make that was loaded with sour cream. If you also want to reduce the cholesterol, purchase yolk-free egg noodles, which are available in most supermarkets. This dish is best when served immediately after preparing rather than made ahead.

8 ounces wide egg noodles

1/2 cup nonfat ricotta cheese

1/2 cup plain yogurt

1/2 cup nonfat cottage cheese

1 (2-ounce) jar diced pimiento, drained

1/2 teaspoon minced garlic

1 tablespoon poppyseeds (see Tip)

1/2 teaspoon hot pepper sauce, or to taste

1/2 teaspoon pepper, or to taste

1/2 cup finely shredded Cheddar cheese

Dash of paprika

GARNISH (OPTIONAL)   sprigs of fresh flat-leaf parsley, steamed broccoli florets or asparagus spears

1. Bring a large pot of water to a boil over high heat; add the noodles. When the water returns to a boil, stir occasionally to separate the noodles. Reduce the heat to medium-high and cook for about 6 to 8 minutes, or according to package instructions, until the noodles are *al dente*.

2. While the noodles are cooking, stir together the remaining ingredients, except the Cheddar cheese and paprika, in a small bowl.

3. When noodles are done, drain well; return to the pot. Add the ricotta mixture and toss over medium heat until heated through. Adjust the seasonings to taste.

4. Pour the mixture into a large microwave-proof dish; top with the Cheddar cheese and paprika. Heat on high in the microwave, for about 3 minutes or until the cheese is melted.

PER SERVING: Cal 131/Prot 9.4g/Carb 13.6g/Fat 4.3g/Chol 27mg/Sod 168mg

TIP

Poppyseeds provide a crunchy texture and nutty flavor. Because they are prone to rancidity, store poppyseeds for up to 6 months in an airtight container in the refrigerator.

chapter 5 *Entrées*

macaroni and cheese with vegetables

Makes 6 servings

This is more interesting than the kind we ate as kids. And it's versatile—add other vegetables of your choice when sautéing the bell pepper and mushrooms. This dish is best when made just before serving.

8 ounces bow tie pasta (farfalle)

3 tablespoons butter, divided

1 tablespoon all-purpose flour

$^3/_4$ cup skim milk

$^1/_2$ cup vegetable stock (see pages xxiv and 3)

$^1/_2$ cup finely shredded Cheddar cheese

$^1/_2$ cup freshly grated Parmesan cheese

1 tablespoon minced fresh flat-leaf parsley

1 teaspoon dried basil

$^1/_4$ teaspoon paprika (see Tip)

$^1/_4$ teaspoon pepper, or to taste

1 red bell pepper, coarsely chopped

1 cup sliced mushrooms

2 medium scallions, sliced

GARNISH (OPTIONAL)   coarsely chopped scallions

1. Bring a large pot of water to a boil over high heat; add the pasta. When the water returns to a boil, stir occasionally to separate the bow ties. Reduce the heat to medium-high and cook for about 12 to 14 minutes, or according to package instructions, until the pasta is *al dente*.

2. While the pasta is cooking, melt 2 tablespoons of the butter in a medium nonstick saucepan over medium heat; add the flour and stir constantly until smooth. Whisk in the milk and stock; whisk constantly until the mixture thickens. Reduce the heat to

low; stir in cheeses, parsley, basil, paprika, and pepper. Continue stirring until the cheese is melted. Remove from the heat; set aside.

3. Melt the remaining 1 tablespoon butter in a large nonstick sauté pan over medium-high heat. Add the bell pepper, mushrooms, and scallions; cook, stirring constantly, for about 5 minutes or until crisp-tender. Remove from the heat.

4. When the noodles are done, drain well. Add to the pan of vegetables and toss; stir in the cheese sauce. Adjust the seasoning to taste.

PER SERVING: Cal 238/Prot 11.5g/Carb 20.5g/Fat 12.2g/Chol 33mg/Sod 312mg

> **TIP**
>
> Paprika, a powder made by grinding aromatic sweet red pepper pods, can range from mild to pungent and hot, and the color from red-orange to deep red. Hungarian paprika is considered by many to be the best. To preserve its color and flavor, store paprika in a cool, dark place for no longer than 6 months.

herbed
macaroni
parmesan

Makes 4 servings

This very simple dish is one of my favorite "emergency" dinners that I make when time is especially limited. Use short cuts or strands of other Italian pastas you might have on hand. When time permits, I expand on the simple recipe and add other vegetables, such as strips of grilled portobello mushrooms (see Tip).

8 ounces elbow macaroni

3 tablespoons butter

$^1/_2$ cup freshly grated Parmesan cheese

1 plum tomato (at room temperature), cut into $^1/_2$-inch cubes

2 tablespoons minced fresh basil (or 2 teaspoons dried basil)

2 tablespoons minced fresh flat-leaf parsley

Dash of pepper, or to taste

TIP

Portobello mushrooms are large dark brown mushrooms with an open flat cap; the tops can measure up to 6 inches in diameter. Because of a long growing cycle, the gills are exposed and moisture evaporates; this concentrates the flavor and creates a dense, meaty texture.

1. Bring a large pot of water to a boil over high heat; add the macaroni. When the water returns to a boil, stir occasionally to separate the macaroni. Reduce the heat to medium-high and cook for about 6 to 8 minutes, or according to package instructions, until the macaroni is *al dente*.

2. When the macaroni is done, drain well; return to the pot. Add the butter; stir until it melts. Add the remaining ingredients and toss. Adjust the seasoning to taste.

PER SERVING: Cal 224/Prot 8.3g/Carb 17.7g/Fat 13.3g/Chol 34mg/Sod 382mg

Asparagus-Cashew Stir-Fry (page 134)

asparagus-cashew
stir-fry

Makes 4 servings

Serve this in the spring when asparagus is at its best.

4 cups cooked rice

Soy-Ginger Sauce

2 tablespoons cold water

2 tablespoons cornstarch

1$\frac{1}{2}$ cups vegetable stock (see pages xxiv and 3) or water

3 tablespoons low-sodium soy sauce

1 tablespoon minced fresh ginger

1 teaspoon dark sesame oil

$\frac{1}{4}$ teaspoon red pepper flakes, or to taste

Dash of ground white pepper, or to taste (see Tip)

To Complete the Recipe

2 tablespoons canola or safflower oil

3 cups asparagus cut into 2-inch lengths

4 medium scallions, coarsely chopped

1 red bell pepper, coarsely chopped

$\frac{1}{2}$ teaspoon minced garlic

1 cup raw cashews

GARNISH (OPTIONAL)   toasted sesame seeds, mandarin orange segments

1. Cook or reheat the rice (see page 5).

2. Stir together the water and cornstarch in a medium bowl until smooth. Whisk in the remaining sauce ingredients; set aside.

3. Heat the oil in a large nonstick skillet or a wok over medium-high heat. Add the asparagus, scallions, bell pepper, and garlic; cook, stirring constantly, for about 5 minutes or until the vegetables are crisp-tender.

4. Reduce the heat to medium. Stir the sauce mixture; pour it over the vegetables and stir gently for about 1 minute or until it is thickened and bubbly. Fold in the cashews. Adjust the seasonings to taste.

5. Serve the stir-fried mixture over individual servings of rice.

PER SERVING: Cal 475/Prot 13.9g/Carb 59.6g/Fat 20.1g/Chol 0mg/Sod 485mg

Variations

- With the cashews, gently fold in about 8 ounces firm or extra-firm tofu cut into ¹/₂-inch cubes.

- Serve the stir-fry over couscous or Chinese wheat-flour noodles rather than rice.

> ### TIP
>
> Berries of the pepper vine are used to produce both black pepper and white pepper. For black pepper, green berries are picked and sun-dried, turning black and shrinking in the process. For white pepper, the berries are allowed to ripen on the vine; they are picked and soaked in water to remove the outer coating, leaving the inner gray-white kernel. These inner kernels are sun-dried to produce white pepper, which is slightly less spicy than black pepper. It is often used in Asian recipes and in light-colored sauces where dark specks of black pepper would stand out.

sweet
and sour
tofu

Makes 6 servings

You can chop the vegetables in advance, but to retain their crisp-tender texture, serve this dish right after preparing. For variety, substitute couscous, Chinese wheat-flour noodles, or buckwheat (soba) noodles for the rice.

4 cups cooked rice

Sweet and Sour Sauce

2 tablespoons cold water

2 tablespoons cornstarch

1 cup pineapple juice

1/3 cup white rice vinegar

2 tablespoons low-sodium soy sauce

3 tablespoons tomato paste (see Tip)

2 tablespoons honey

1 tablespoon minced fresh ginger

Dash of ground white pepper, or to taste

To Complete the Recipe

2 tablespoons canola or safflower oil

1 red bell pepper, cut lengthwise into 1/4-inch-wide strips

1 green bell pepper, cut lengthwise into 1/4-inch-wide strips

2 carrots, thinly sliced

1 medium onion, cut into 1/4-inch-wide strips

1/2 teaspoon minced garlic

12 ounces firm or extra-firm tofu, cut into 1/2-inch cubes

1 large tomato, cut into wedges

1 (8-ounce) can unsweetened pineapple chunks, drained

2 tablespoons toasted sesame seeds

GARNISH (OPTIONAL)   scallion curls (see Tip, page 123), sprigs of fresh cilantro

1. Cook or reheat the rice (see page 5).

2. Stir together the water and cornstarch in a medium bowl until smooth. Whisk in the remaining sauce ingredients; set aside.

3. Heat the oil in a large nonstick skillet or wok over medium-high heat. Add the bell peppers, carrots, onion, and garlic; cook, stirring constantly, for about 5 minutes or until the carrots are crisp-tender.

4. Reduce the heat to medium. Stir the sauce mixture; pour it over vegetables. Stir for about 1 minute or until the sauce thickens. Gently stir in the tofu, tomato, and pineapple. Adjust the seasoning to taste.

5. Spoon the vegetable mixture over individual servings of rice; sprinkle with sesame seeds.

PER SERVING: Cal 359/Prot 7.3g/Carb 63.7g/Fat 8.3g/Chol 0mg/Sod 313mg

Variation

•   Substitute other vegetables for the bell peppers or carrots (up to 3 cups total). Try broccoli florets, cut asparagus, or sliced mushrooms.

TIP

Tomato paste is available in tubes at many groceries and specialty stores. It is ideal for recipes calling for less than a 6-ounce can.

vegetable
curry

Makes 6 servings

For protein, fold in cubes of firm or extra-firm tofu with the vegetables. To make a more substantial meal for guests, accompany this dish with Mixed Fruit Chutney (page 15) and a green salad tossed with Apple Salad Dressing (page 73).

4 cups cooked rice

1 cup cauliflower florets

1 cup broccoli florets

2 carrots, sliced

1 red bell pepper, cut into 1-inch-long by $1/2$-inch-wide pieces

1 medium onion, cut into wedges

1 cup frozen peas (preferably baby peas), thawed

Curry Sauce

2 tablespoons canola or safflower oil

2 tablespoons curry powder

2 tablespoons minced fresh ginger

$1^1/2$ teaspoons minced garlic

1 small hot red chili pepper, minced (or $1/2$ teaspoon red pepper flakes), or to taste

$1/2$ cup vegetable stock (see pages xxiv and 3)

2 tablespoons fresh lime juice

To Complete the Recipe

2 tomatoes (at room temperature), cut into wedges (see Tip)

000000000000000000GARNISH (OPTIONAL)   toasted sesame seeds, unsalted dry-roasted peanuts, sprigs of fresh cilantro

1. Cook or reheat the rice (see page 5).

2. Put the cauliflower, broccoli, and carrots into a large microwave-proof dish; add about ¼ cup water. Cover and microwave on high for about 6 minutes or until the vegetables are crisp-tender. Add the bell pepper, onion, and peas for the last 2 minutes (or cook the vegetables in a stovetop steamer for about 6 minutes).

3. Meanwhile, heat the oil for the sauce in a large saucepan over medium-high heat. Add the curry powder, ginger, garlic, and chili pepper (if using). Cook, stirring constantly, for about 2 minutes or until aromatic. Add the vegetable stock. Increase the heat to high; bring the sauce to a boil. Cook, uncovered, for about 3 minutes or until the sauce is somewhat reduced and slightly thickened. Remove from the heat. Stir in the lime juice and red pepper flakes (if using).

4. When the vegetables are done, drain well. Add the vegetables and the tomato wedges to the sauce and toss gently. Adjust the seasoning to taste.

5. Serve the vegetables and sauce over individual servings of rice.

PER SERVING: Cal 280/Prot 7.3g/Carb 48.6g/Fat 6.3g/Chol 0mg/Sod 162mg

Variations

- Substitute other vegetables for the cauliflower, broccoli, carrots, or bell pepper (up to 4 cups total). Try halved new potatoes or sliced mushrooms.

- Substitute Chinese wheat-flour noodles or buckwheat (soba) noodles for the rice.

TIP

Because cold temperatures reduce the flavor of tomatoes and can make their texture mealy, don't store them in the refrigerator. Instead, store them on the counter at room temperature, where they will become redder, softer, juicier, and tastier as they ripen. Once fully ripened, use tomatoes within 2 days.

vegetable
stir-fry
with **ginger sauce**

Makes 4 servings

The mouthwatering flavor of Ginger Sauce makes this one of my favorite dishes for entertaining. You can use just about any vegetables; begin by stir-frying the firmest vegetables first, followed by those that are softer and more tender, so that they will all reach a perfect crisp-tender texture.

4 cups cooked rice

1 cup Ginger Sauce (page 24)

3 tablespoons canola or safflower oil

2 carrots, thinly sliced on the diagonal

1 medium onion, thinly sliced

1/2 teaspoon minced garlic

4 ribs bok choy, thinly sliced (also shred green tops); (see Tip)

1 1/2 cups sliced mushrooms

1 red bell pepper, cut lengthwise into 1/4-inch-wide strips

1 (8-ounce) can bamboo shoots, drained and rinsed

1 cup frozen peas (preferably baby peas), thawed

8 ounces firm or extra-firm tofu, cut into 1/2-inch cubes

GARNISH (OPTIONAL)   toasted sesame seeds, toasted sliced almonds, scallion curls (see Tip, page 123)

1. Cook or reheat the rice (see page 5).

2. Prepare the Ginger Sauce; while it is simmering, prepare the stir-fry ingredients. Remove the sauce from the heat and cover.

3. Heat the oil in a large nonstick skillet or wok over medium-high heat. Add the carrots; stir-fry for about 2 minutes. Add onion and garlic; continue to stir-fry for 2 more minutes. Add the remaining ingredients, except the tofu; stir-fry for about 4 more minutes or until the carrrots and bok choy are crisp-tender. Gently fold in the tofu; allow to stand for about 1 minute.

4. Spoon the stir-fried vegetables over individual servings of rice. Drizzle with about half of the Ginger Sauce. Pass the remaining Ginger Sauce in a small container at the table.

PER SERVING: Cal 544/Prot 14.6g/Carb 89.2g/Fat 14.3g/Chol 0mg/Sod 564mg

Variations

- To serve this dish as an appetizer: Finely chop all of the vegetables, stir-fry just until crisp-tender. Spoon tablespoon-size mounds of the vegetables on endive leaves; drizzle each with a small amount of the Ginger Sauce.

- Substitute 1 cup Orange-Tahini Sauce (page 23) for the Ginger Sauce.

> ### TIP
>
> Bok choy should have bright dark green, unwilted leaves attached to crisp lighter green unblemished stalks; both the leaves and stalks are edible cooked or raw. Store bok choy for up to 3 days in a plastic bag in the refrigerator.

asian
stir-fried
rice

Makes 4 servings

I prefer using brown rice for this recipe because of its firm texture and nutty flavor. Sometimes I add some wild rice.

TIPS

- Scallions, also called green onions or spring onions, are delicately flavored members of the onion family. They come from the thinnings of immature onion bulbs as well as certain kinds of onions that produce long, thin stems.

- The leaves should be bright green and firm; the white bulbs should be firm and unblemished. Both parts can be used in recipes calling for scallions.

- The size varies from very slender to large and thick; as a rule, the more slender the bottoms, the sweeter the flavor.

- Store scallions for up to 1 week, wrapped in a plastic bag, in the vegetable crisper section of the refrigerator.

3 tablespoons canola or
  safflower oil, divided

2 eggs, lightly beaten

1 cup sliced mushrooms

1 rib celery, chopped

1/2 cup fresh bean sprouts

1/2 cup alfalfa sprouts

2 medium scallions, chopped (see Tips)

2 cups cooked rice

1 cup frozen peas (preferably baby peas),
  thawed

2 tablespoons low-sodium soy sauce

Dash of ground white pepper, or to taste

GARNISH (OPTIONAL)   red bell pepper strips

1. Heat 1 tablespoon of the oil in a large nonstick skillet or wok over medium heat; add the eggs. Scramble until eggs are almost set; transfer them to a bowl, cover to keep warm, and set aside.

2. Heat the remaining oil in the same pan. Add the mushrooms, celery, sprouts, and scallions; cook, stirring constantly, for about 2 minutes. Add the rice; cook for about 3 minutes. Add the scrambled eggs and the remaining ingredients; stir gently until heated through. Adjust the seasoning to taste.

PER SERVING: Cal 281/Prot 8.5g/Carb 31g/Fat 13.7g/Chol 106mg/Sod 568mg

ADVANCE PREPARATION   This dish will keep for up to 2 days in a covered container in the refrigerator.

asian
rice
and
vegetable skillet

Makes 4 servings

Here's a delicious catch-all for using the odds and ends of vegetables in your refrigerator. Complement it with a spinach salad tossed with Honey-Poppyseed Dressing (page 69).

2 tablespoons canola or safflower oil

$1/2$ cup coarsely chopped onion

1 carrot, coarsely chopped (see Tips)

2 stalks bok choy, coarsely chopped (also shred green tops)

$1/2$ red bell pepper, coarsely chopped

1 cup stemmed snow peas

1 cup fresh bean sprouts

1 cup shredded stemmed spinach leaves

2 cups cooked brown rice

$1/4$ cup slivered almonds

2 tablespoons low-sodium soy sauce

$1/2$ teaspoon pepper, or to taste

2 eggs, lightly beaten

GARNISH (OPTIONAL)   toasted sesame seeds

1. Heat the oil in a large skillet over medium-high heat. Add the onion and carrot; cook, stirring constantly, for about 3 minutes or until the onion is tender. Add the bok choy, bell pepper, snow peas, bean sprouts, and spinach as they are prepared. Cook, stirring occasionally, for about 5 minutes or until the spinach is wilted and the other vegetables are crisp-tender.

2. Stir in the rice, almonds, soy sauce, and pepper. Then add the eggs; cook, stirring constantly, for about 4 minutes or until the eggs are lightly set. Adjust the seasoning to taste.

TIPS

- The best carrots are young and slender; avoid buying carrots with cracks or root growth.

- If purchased with the greens attached, remove the greenery as soon as possible because it robs carrots of both vitamins and moisture.

- Store carrots in a plastic bag in the vegetable drawer in your refrigerator.

PER SERVING: Cal 298/Prot 10.1g/Carb 33.6/Fat 13.7g/Chol 106mg/Sod 422mg

chef's
garden
skillet

Makes 6 servings

This is a nice easygoing dish for a family dinner on a busy weeknight, because, if necessary, you can keep it warm in a covered skillet. Serve a green salad tossed with Tangy Honey-Mustard Dressing (page 71).

2 cups broccoli florets

2 carrots, thinly sliced

1 small zucchini, sliced

1/2 cup frozen peas (preferably baby peas), thawed

1 cup nonfat ricotta cheese

2 tablespoons freshly grated Parmesan cheese

1 tablespoon butter

1/4 cup slivered almonds

1/4 cup finely chopped onion

1/2 teaspoon minced garlic

2 cups cooked rice

1 tablespoon low-sodium soy sauce

1 (8-ounce) can tomato sauce

1 tablespoon minced fresh flat-leaf parsley

1 teaspoon dried oregano

1/2 teaspoon pepper, or to taste

1 cup shredded mozzarella cheese

Dash of paprika

1. Put the broccoli, carrot, zucchini, and peas into a large microwave-proof dish; add about 1/4 cup water. Cover and microwave on high for about 5 minutes or until the vegetables are crisp-tender. (Or cook the vegetables in a stovetop steamer for about 5 minutes.)

2. Meanwhile, combine the ricotta and Parmesan cheese in a small bowl.

3. Melt the butter in a large nonstick sauté pan over medium-high heat. Add the almonds, onion, and garlic. Cook, stirring occasionally, for about 2 minutes or until the almonds are lightly browned and the onion is tender. Stir in the rice and soy sauce. Use the back of a large spoon to smooth out the top of the mixture. Drop on spoonfuls of the ricotta mixture. Cover and reduce the heat to medium.

4. When the vegetables are done, drain well. Transfer them to a large bowl; stir in the tomato sauce, parsley, oregano, and pepper. Adjust the seasoning to taste. Spread over the ricotta layer in the skillet. Top with the mozzarella cheese and sprinkle with paprika. Cover and heat for about 5 minutes or until the cheese is melted.

PER SERVING: Cal 272/Prot 15.3g/Carb 33.2g/Fat 8.7g/Chol 23mg/Sod 534mg

vegetarian
tacos

Makes 4 servings

I usually arrange the taco filling and condiments buffet-fashion and allow family or guests to assemble their own taco.

2 tablespoons canola or safflower oil

3 cups sliced mushrooms

1 medium zucchini, sliced

1 carrot, coarsely shredded

1/4 cup coarsely chopped onion

1/2 teaspoon minced garlic

2 tomatoes, cut into 1/2-inch cubes
   (about 1 1/2 cups)

1 (8-ounce) can tomato sauce

1 tablespoon chili powder (see Tip)

1/4 teaspoon ground cumin

Dash of hot pepper sauce, or to taste

8 packaged taco shells

2 cups shredded Cheddar cheese

1/4 head lettuce, finely shredded

Bottled taco hot sauce

GARNISH (OPTIONAL)   orange slices

1. Preheat the oven to 350°F.

2. Heat the oil in a large nonstick sauté pan over medium-high heat. Stir in the mushrooms, zucchini, carrot, onion, and garlic; cook, stirring occasionally, for about 4 minutes or until the zucchini is crisp-tender. Stir in about half of the tomatoes, tomato sauce, chili powder, cumin, and hot pepper sauce. Reduce the heat to medium; cover and cook for about 5 minutes. Adjust the seasoning to taste.

3. Meanwhile, arrange the taco shells on a baking sheet; warm in the oven for about 5 minutes.

4. To serve, spoon the vegetable mixture into the taco shells. Top with cheese, lettuce, and the remaining tomato. Drizzle with taco sauce.

PER SERVING: Cal 499/Prot 19.7g/Carb 32.8g/Fat 32.1g/Chol 60mg/Sod 838mg

ADVANCE PREPARATION   The taco filling will keep for up to 3 days in a covered container in the refrigerator; reheat the filling and assemble the tacos just before serving.

Variations

- While the taco filling is heating, stir in beans, such as kidney or garbanzo beans.

- Substitute Tomato Hot Sauce (page 156) for the bottled taco hot sauce.

- Instead of filling taco shells, use the Vegetarian Taco mixture as a filling for omelets or pita bread. Or, use as a topping for English muffins: Spread the mixture on toasted English muffin halves, sprinkle with cheese, and broil for a few minutes to melt the cheese.

> **TIP**
>
> If you want to make your chili powder hotter, add a dash of cayenne pepper.

couscous
with egg sauce
and garden vegetables

Makes 4 servings

This quick-to-prepare egg sauce also makes a pleasant topping for steamed vegetables.

$1^1/_2$ cups vegetable stock (see pages xxiv and 3) or water

$1^1/_2$ cups couscous

16 asparagus spears

Egg Sauce

$1^1/_2$ cups skim milk

2 hard-cooked eggs (see Tip)

3 tablespoons butter

$^1/_2$ teaspoon minced garlic

3 tablespoons all-purpose flour

2 tablespoons minced fresh flat-leaf parsley

2 teaspoons low-sodium soy sauce

$^1/_4$ teaspoon powdered mustard

Dash of ground white pepper, or to taste

GARNISH (OPTIONAL)   dash of paprika

1. Heat the stock or water, until hot but not boiling, in a small saucepan over medium-high heat. Remove the pan from the heat; stir in the couscous. Let stand, covered, for about 5 to 10 minutes or until the liquid is completely absorbed.

2. Meanwhile, put the asparagus into a medium microwave-proof dish; add about $^1/_4$ cup water. Cover and microwave on high for about 4 minutes or until the vegetables are crisp-tender. (Or cook the asparagus for about 4 minutes in a stovetop steamer.)

3. Meanwhile, process the milk and eggs in a blender until smooth; set aside.

4. Melt the butter in a medium saucepan over medium heat; add the garlic and cook, stirring constantly, for about 1 minute or until softened. Add the flour and stir constantly until smooth. Add the milk mixture; whisk constantly until the sauce thickens. Stir in the remaining sauce ingredients. Adjust the seasoning to taste.

5. When the couscous is softened, fluff it with a fork. When the asparagus is done, drain well.

6. To assemble each serving, spread couscous on a plate; top with 4 asparagus spears. Drizzle with sauce.

PER SERVING: Cal 319/Prot 15g/Carb 36.2g/Fat 12.7g/Chol 132mg/Sod 317mg

ADVANCE PREPARATION   This sauce will keep for up to 2 days in a covered container in the refrigerator. Reheat the sauce, prepare the couscous and asparagus, and assemble the dish just before serving.

TIP

To hard-cook eggs: For best results, place them in a single layer in a pan and cover with at least 1 inch of cold water. Cover pan and bring the water to a full rolling boil over medium-high heat. Remove the pan from the heat, and let the eggs stand in the water, covered, for about 15 minutes for large eggs. (For larger or smaller eggs, adjust the time up or down by about 3 minutes for each size variation.)

Drain off the hot water and immediately cover the eggs with cold water; let stand until the eggs are completely cool. This cooling process prevents darkening around the yolk. (If it does occur, the color is harmless and does not alter the nutritional value or flavor of the egg.) This method of quick cooling also causes the eggs to contract, making them easier to peel. Refrigerate hard-cooked eggs for up to 1 week.

savory
nut
burgers

Makes 4 servings

Serve these vegetarian burgers on buns with lettuce, tomato slices, melted cheese, and ketchup or the zesty homemade mustard on page 13. Or serve the burgers without bread and top with sauce, such as Zesty Tomato Sauce (page 20), Tomato-Garlic Sauce (page 21), or Tomato-Yogurt Sauce (page 22).

1 cup finely chopped walnuts, preferably toasted

$1/2$ cup toasted wheat germ

$1/4$ cup nonfat cottage cheese

1 egg, lightly beaten

2 tablespoons sesame seeds

1 tablespoon minced fresh flat-leaf parsley

1 tablespoon finely chopped onion

1 teaspoon minced garlic

1 teaspoon low-sodium soy sauce

$1/4$ teaspoon dried thyme

1 tablespoon canola or safflower oil

1. Stir together all of the ingredients, except the oil, in a medium bowl. Form the mixture into 4 patties about 4 inches in diameter and $1/2$-inch thick.

2. Heat the oil in a large nonstick skillet over medium-high heat. Cook the patties for about 3 minutes on each side or until lightly browned.

PER SERVING: Cal 278/Prot 9.5g/Carb 10.1g/Fat 22.2g/Chol 54mg/Sod 151mg

ADVANCE PREPARATION   The Savory Nut Burger mixture can be mixed in advance; cover and refrigerate for up to 1 day. Cook the patties just before serving.

Variations

- Substitute dry bread crumbs for the wheat germ.

- Form the burger mixture into walnut-sized balls; either sauté them until lightly browned or arrange the balls on a baking sheet and bake in a 350°F oven for about 8 minutes. Stir into Marinara Sauce (page 19) to serve over pasta or use as an appetizer accompanied by Zesty Tomato Sauce (page 20) or Peanut Sauce (page 25).

- To make sloppy Joes: Omit the wheat germ. Sauté the burger mixture in a large nonstick skillet over medium-high heat until lightly browned. Stir in 1/2 cup tomato sauce and heat through. Serve on buns or stuffed into pita bread pockets.

noodle **omelet**

Makes 4 servings

Adding noodles makes an omelet more substantial. I use fine egg noodles because they are quick to prepare and have a tender texture. Or you can substitute cooked rice for the noodles and follow the same cooking procedure. If you'd like, serve the omelet with your choice of filling and sauce, such as the suggestions on page 153.

$1/2$ cup fine egg noodles	3 tablespoons cold water
6 eggs	2 tablespoons butter

1. Bring a small saucepan of water to a boil over high heat; add the noodles. When the water returns to a boil, stir occasionally to separate the noodles. Reduce the heat to medium-high and cook for about 3 to 5 minutes, or according to package directions, until the noodles are *al dente*.

2. While the noodles are cooking, lightly beat the eggs and water with a fork or whisk in a medium bowl just long enough to combine. When the noodles are done, drain well. Stir them into the egg mixture.

3. Heat the butter in a large nonstick skillet over medium-high heat until it bubbles. Swirl it to coat the pan, then pour in egg mixture. As the edges become firm, push them toward the center, tilting the pan so that the uncooked portions can flow to the hot pan surface.

4. While the egg is still moist (but not runny), reduce the heat to low. Spread the filling along the center third of the omelet, perpendicular to the pan handle. Slip a spatula under the third nearest the handle and fold it over the filling. Cover the pan and heat for about 2 minutes.

5. Slide the omelet onto a serving plate by sliding the outermost third onto the plate, then lift the pan handle to roll the remainder over so the omelet lands seam side down. Cut into quarters to serve.

PER SERVING (OMELET ONLY): Cal 178/Prot 10.1g/Carb 4.3g/Fat 13.4g/Chol 339mg/Sod 154mg

Other Omelets

- Fill any omelet with Basil Pesto (page 16) or Spinach Parsley Pesto (page 18); top with Herbed Tomato Sauce (page 76).

- Fill any omelet with steamed or sautéed vegetables and top with one of the following sauces: Garlic-Tomato Sauce (page 21), Tomato-Yogurt Sauce (page 22), Zesty Tomato Sauce (page 20), or Ginger Sauce (page 24).

> **TIP**
>
> For all the filled omelets, prepare the sauce and filling first, then the omelet—a French Omelet (page 10), Fluffy Omelet (page 11), or Noodle Omelet (page 152).

tomato-ricotta
omelet

Makes 4 servings

Use this tasty combination of sauce and filling with your choice of omelet: French Omelet (page 10), used for the nutrition analysis, or Noodle Omelet (page 152).

Herbed Tomato Sauce (page 76)

Ricotta Filling

³/₄ cup nonfat ricotta cheese (at room
   temperature)

1 tablespoon skim milk

1 teaspoon minced fresh flat-leaf parsley

1 teaspoon dried tarragon

¹/₄ teaspoon pepper

GARNISH (OPTIONAL)   toasted pine nuts, freshly grated Parmesan cheese, steamed asparagus tips, sprigs of fresh basil

1. Prepare the Herbed Tomato Sauce; set aside.

2. Stir together the filling ingredients in a medium bowl.

3. Make your choice of omelet.

4. Fill the omelet with Ricotta Filling. Cover to heat for 1 to 2 minutes. Turn out onto a serving dish as described in the recipe for your choice of omelet. Top the omelet with Herbed Tomato Sauce. Cut into 4 portions.

PER SERVING: Cal 252/Prot 16.9g/Carb 7.6g/Fat 16.7g/Chol 431mg/Sod 502mg

Guacamole Omelet with Tomato Hot Sauce

guacamole omelet
with tomato
hot sauce

Makes 4 servings

Serve this omelet with a Mexican flair for brunch, lunch, or dinner. At another time, serve the Guacamole Filling as an appetizer dip for Pita Crisps (page 63), taco chips, or an assortment of raw vegetables.

Tomato Hot Sauce

1 (15-ounce) can tomato sauce

$1/4$ teaspoon hot pepper sauce

1 teaspoon ground coriander

$1/2$ teaspoon pepper

$1/4$ teaspoon ground cumin

Dash of red pepper flakes, or to taste

Guacamole Filling

2 avocados (at room temperature), peeled and halved (see Tips)

3 tablespoons nonfat plain yogurt

2 tablespoons fresh lemon or lime juice

1 tablespoon coarsely chopped onion

Dash of hot pepper sauce, or to taste

Dash of pepper, or to taste

To Complete the Recipe

8 eggs

$1/4$ cup cold water

2 tablespoons butter

GARNISH (OPTIONAL)   tomato slices, alfalfa sprouts, orange wedges, plain yogurt or nonfat sour cream

1. Stir together the sauce ingredients in a small saucepan; cover and heat, stirring occasionally, over low heat. Remove from the heat; set aside.

2. Meanwhile, process all of the filling ingredients in a food processor until smooth. Adjust the seasoning to taste. Cover and set aside.

3. To prepare the omelet, lightly beat the eggs and water with a fork or whisk in a medium bowl just long enough to combine.

4. Heat the butter in a large nonstick skillet over medium-high heat until it bubbles. Swirl it to coat the pan, then pour in egg mixture. As the edges become firm, push them toward the center, tilting the pan so that the uncooked portions can flow to the hot pan surface.

5. While the egg is still moist (but not runny), reduce the heat to low. Spread the avocado filling along the center third of the omelet, perpendicular to the pan handle. Slip a spatula under the third nearest the handle and fold it over the filling. Cover the pan and heat for about 2 minutes.

6. Slide the omelet onto a serving plate by sliding the outermost third onto a large platter, then lift the pan handle to roll the remainder over so the omelet lands seam-side down.

7. Slice the omelet into 4 portions; transfer them to individual serving plates. Spoon about ¼ cup of the warm sauce over each serving.

PER SERVING: Cal 279/Prot 15.9g/Carb 13.5g/Fat 17.1g/Chol 429mg/Sod 993mg

ADVANCE PREPARATION   The Tomato Hot Sauce will keep for up to 5 days in a closed container in the refrigerator; reheat before serving. Make the Guacamole Filling no more than 1 hour before serving; cover and hold at room temperature.

TIPS

- The two most common varieties of avocados are the Fuerte, which has a smooth green skin, and the pebbly textured, almost black Haas, which I prefer.

- Most avocados require a few days of ripening after purchasing; place them in a pierced paper bag at room temperature for a day or two to speed up the process. The avocados will yield to gentle pressure when they are ripe and ready to use. Store ripe avocados in the refrigerator for up to 5 days.

- Once cut and exposed to air, avocado flesh discolors rapidly; to minimize this, coat the cut surfaces with lime or lemon juice and add these juices to recipes calling for avocados.

curry-chutney
omelet

Makes 4 servings

Nearly every vegetable goes with the vibrant flavor of curry powder. To make the omelet more substantial, cook thin slices of new potatoes with the mushrooms, or simply stir in some baby peas when the sauce is completed. Use this with French Omelet (page 10), used for the nutrition analysis, Fluffy Omelet (page 11), or Noodle Omelet (page 152).

Curry Sauce

2 tablespoons butter

1 cup sliced mushrooms

1 carrot, finely grated

2 tablespoons minced onion

1 tablespoon curry powder

1¼ cups skim milk

¼ teaspoon pepper

⅛ teaspoon ground cumin

1 tablespoon water

1 tablespoon cornstarch

¼ cup apple juice

Filling

⅓ cup Mixed Fruit Chutney (page 15)

GARNISH (OPTIONAL)   sprigs of fresh flat-leaf parsley or cilantro (see Tip)

1. Heat the butter in a medium saucepan over medium-high heat; add the mushrooms, carrot, onion, and curry powder. Cook, stirring occasionally, for about 3 minutes or until the vegetables are tender. Reduce the heat to medium. Stir in the milk, pepper, and cumin; heat, stirring occasionally, until warm.

2. Stir together the water and cornstarch in a measuring cup until smooth. Stir in the apple juice. Pour into the curry mixture. Reduce the heat to low; cook, stirring constantly, for about 3 minutes or until the sauce thickens. Cover and remove from the heat.

3. Make your choice of omelet.

4. Fill the omelet with Mixed Fruit Chutney. Top with the Curry Sauce.

PER SERVING: Cal 266/Prot 15.9g/Carb 14.5g/Fat 16.1g/Chol 442mg/Sod 231mg

ADVANCE PREPARATION   The Curry Sauce will keep for up to 1 day in a covered container in the refrigerator; reheat to serve. Bring the chutney to room temperature before assembling the omelet.

TIP

Cilantro, often sold as "fresh coriander" or "Chinese parsley," is commonly used for its distinctive pungent flavor and aroma in Thai, Vietnamese, Asian, Indian, and Mexican cuisines. The dried leaves lack fresh cilantro's distinctive flavor and are an unacceptable substitution.

italian
garden
frittata

Makes 4 servings

Frittatas are to Italians what omelets are to the French. The ingredients may be the same, but the difference is in the cooking method. In a frittata the filling is mixed with the eggs, and the entire mixture is cooked together and left open-faced. You can serve this as-is or top it with a sauce such as Marinara Sauce (page 19), Herbed Tomato Sauce (page 76), Garlic-Tomato Sauce (page 21), or Tomato-Yogurt Sauce (page 22).

3 tablespoons butter

1 cup sliced mushrooms (see Tips)

1 cup sliced zucchini

1/2 red bell pepper, cut into julienne strips

1/2 green bell pepper, cut into julienne strips

1/4 cup coarsely chopped onion

1/2 teaspoon minced garlic

4 eggs, lightly beaten

2 tablespoons water

3/4 cup freshly grated Parmesan cheese, divided

Dash of pepper

Dash of dried basil

Dash of dried oregano

GARNISH (OPTIONAL)   freshly ground black pepper, paprika, sprigs of fresh basil

1. Heat the butter in a large nonstick skillet over medium-high heat; add the mushrooms, zucchini, bell peppers, onion, and garlic. Cook, stirring occasionally, for about 4 minutes or until the vegetables are tender.

2. Meanwhile, lightly beat the eggs and water with a fork or whisk in a medium bowl just long enough to combine. Whisk in ¹⁄₄ cup of the Parmesan cheese and the remaining ingredients. Pour the mixture over the cooked vegetables in the skillet. Tilt the pan cover over the pan, allowing the steam to escape. Cook for about 6 to 8 minutes or until the eggs are set.

3. Serve the frittata directly from the skillet or loosen it around the edges with a spatula and slide the frittata onto a serving platter. Sprinkle with the remaining Parmesan cheese and slice into wedges for serving.

PER SERVING: Cal 264/Prot 15.3g/Carb 5.9g/Fat 19.9g/Chol 251mg/Sod 585mg

ADVANCE PREPARATION   Prepare this dish just before serving, unless you plan to serve it chilled or at room temperature as an appetizer.

Variations

- Substitute other vegetables for the mushrooms, zucchini, or bell peppers (up to 3 cups total). Try shredded carrots, sliced potatoes, cut asparagus, or broccoli florets.

- To serve as an appetizer, chop the vegetables more finely and cut the frittata into thin wedges for serving warm or at room temperature; accompany with Herbed Tomato Sauce (page 76).

TIPS

- Refrigerate mushrooms for up to 4 days in a paper bag or basket so air can circulate around them.

- To clean, simply brush with a mushroom brush or wipe with a moist paper towel. If necessary, rinse them quickly; mushrooms are very absorbent and should never soak in water.

- Before using, cut off any woody stems and trim the bottoms off tender stems.

chapter 6

Desserts

ELEGANT FINALES, THESE DESSERTS RUN THE GAMUT

from luscious chocolate to dazzling fresh sorbets. Most

of the recipes use very little sugar (some none at all),

just a touch of fat, an egg or two, yet they *taste* indulgent.

All are ready in little time, but no one need know how

simple they are or how nutritious.

Seasonal fruit in its prime is perhaps the purest pleasure. Serve pears with a sprinkling of ginger, tart apples with a dusting of ground cinnamon or nutmeg, wedges of crenshaw melon with a squeeze of fresh lime juice—light touches that take no more than a minute.

Fresh fruit is sweetest when fully ripe. Most soft fruit is shipped while still hard. Fruit ripening bowls (clear-plastic bowls with domed, vented lids), available at most supermarkets or gourmet shops, can help speed the ripening along.

Cooking fresh fruit transforms the taste and texture creating a marvelous base for a variety of sauces. Warm baked, poached, or stewed fruit not only makes a luscious dessert but also can be a delectable addition to brunch.

Quick sorbets can be made from frozen fruit. Try puréeing frozen bananas; the creamy, smooth texture is like rich gourmet ice cream without the fat. I like to keep frozen fruit on hand for healthful snacks and speedy desserts.

Make your desserts a visual feast. Elevate a humble fruit compote by serving it in a long-stemmed goblet garnished with a sprig of mint. Present sliced fruit on pretty platters laced with fresh mint leaves. Enjoy, relax, these are just desserts.

maple
oranges
amandine

Makes 4 servings

If this sounds too easy to be good, I think you will be pleasantly surprised. It's a favorite at my house for dessert, breakfast, and snacks.

1/4 cup fresh orange juice

1/4 cup pure maple syrup

4 oranges (preferably chilled), peeled and
   cut into 1/2-inch cubes (see Tip)

1/4 cup slivered almonds, preferably toasted

> ### TIP
>
> Color is not a sure guide to choosing oranges. Oranges that are heavy for their size and have relatively smooth skins will be the juiciest.

GARNISH (OPTIONAL)   sprigs of fresh mint

1. Stir together the orange juice and maple syrup in a measuring cup; toss with the oranges in a medium bowl.

2. Spoon the oranges with juice into dessert bowls; top with almonds.

PER SERVING: Cal 143/Prot 3.2g/Carb 24.2g/Fat 3.7g/Chol 0mg/Sod 1mg

ADVANCE PREPARATION   This dish will keep for up to 2 days in a covered container in the refrigerator.

Variation

- Substitute pears for oranges; serve immediately after preparing.

vanilla **poached** pears

Makes 4 servings

Poached pears are stunning on their own, but serving them with Maple Hot Chocolate Sauce (page 188), Honey-Raspberry Sauce (page 189), or Orange-Raisin Sauce (page 172) will make this dessert especially memorable. (I often place the pears atop sauce that has been poured onto the dessert plate or drizzle the sauce over the pears.)

2 tablespoons pure vanilla extract

2 tablespoons honey

4 pears (at room temperature), peeled and cored (see Tips)

GARNISH (OPTIONAL)   toasted finely chopped pecans or sliced almonds, toasted wheat germ, sprigs of fresh mint

1. Fill a Dutch oven or $3^1/_2$- to 5-quart saucepan halfway with water; bring to a boil over high heat. Stir in the vanilla and honey, then add the pears. When the water returns to a boil, reduce the heat to medium-high; cook the pears for about 10 minutes or until fork-tender but not soft.

2. Use a slotted spoon to transfer the pears to a plate. Discard the poaching liquid.

PER SERVING: Cal 152/Prot .7g/Carb 34.7g/Fat .7g/Chol 0mg/Sod 1mg

ADVANCE PREPARATION   To serve warm, poach the pears and serve immediately. To serve chilled, poach the pears in advance; allow to cool, then cover and refrigerate for up to 6 hours.

Variations

- Substitute pure maple syrup for the honey.

- If you prefer, poach the pears with the stems and cores intact.

- Stuff the centers of the pears with this filling: Process $^1/_4$ cup almonds, $^1/_4$ cup light raisins, and 2 tablespoons honey in a food processor until the mixture is blended together but not smooth.

TIPS

- Buy pears when they are firm, but not rock-hard, and ripen them on your kitchen counter in a paper bag; this may require 2 to 7 days. Most pears do not show ripeness with a color change because they ripen from the inside out; the stem ends yielding slightly to pressure indicate ripeness. Once ripe, pears will keep for 3 to 5 days in the refrigerator.

- When you peel pears and peaches, treat them like apples. To prevent discoloration, as soon as they are peeled, drop them into water containing lemon, lime, or orange juice.

- Poaching time depends on the ripeness of the pears. It's best to begin with room-temperature pears that are ripe but still firm.

Vanilla-Poached Pears with
Maple Hot Chocolate Sauce (page 166)

baked **peaches**
with chutney dressing

Makes 4 servings

If you don't have time to make your own chutney, select one of the many high-quality commercially-prepared varieties available at the supermarket. You can also substitute canned peach halves if fresh peaches are out of season.

2 peaches (at room temperature), peeled, pitted, and halved (see Tips)

¹/₄ cup Mixed Fruit Chutney (page 15)

GARNISH (OPTIONAL) finely chopped pecans, toasted wheat germ

1. Preheat the oven to 350°F.

2. Arrange the peach halves, cut sides up, on an ungreased baking sheet. Top each with 1 tablespoon chutney.

3. Bake for 10 minutes or until the peaches are tender and the chutney is warm.

PER SERVING: Cal 50/Prot .5g/Carb 11.3g/Fat .1g/Chol 0mg/ Sod 1mg

ADVANCE PREPARATION To serve warm, bake the peaches and serve immediately. To serve chilled, bake the peaches in advance; allow to cool, then cover and refrigerate for up to 6 hours.

TIPS

- Choose peaches that are firm to slightly soft with a yellow or creamy skin color.

- To speed up ripening, put peaches in a paper bag with an apple and let stand at room temperature for 2 to 3 days. When fully ripe, keep peaches in a sealed bag in the refrigerator; use within a few days.

fluffy **strawberry omelet**
with nectarine sauce

Makes 4 servings

This is really something special. It's a bit too substantial for dessert after a large meal, but just right to serve for a summer brunch with tall glasses of fresh-squeezed orange juice. Or serve it as a protein-rich snack. The Nectarine Sauce (or strawberry variation) makes a nonfat fruity sauce for frozen yogurt or ice cream.

4 eggs, separated	1 teaspoon pure vanilla extract
1 tablespoon powdered sugar	1 tablespoon butter

Nectarine Sauce

1 large nectarine (at room temperature), peeled and quartered	2 tablespoons fresh orange juice
	1 tablespoon honey, or as needed

To Complete the Recipe

1 cup sliced strawberries (at room temperature); (see Tip)

GARNISH (OPTIONAL)   kiwi slices

1. Preheat the oven to 325°F.

2. In a small mixing bowl, use an electric mixer to beat the egg whites until foamy. Gradually add the powdered sugar and continue beating until stiff peaks form.

3. In a separate bowl, beat the egg yolks until thick and lemon-colored. Fold the yolks into the whites until well combined. Fold in the vanilla.

170

4. Melt the butter in a large oven-proof skillet over medium-high heat. Pour in the egg mixture and cook for about 5 minutes or until the bottom of the omelet is lightly browned. Transfer the pan to the oven and bake the omelet for 5 to 6 minutes or until a knife inserted in the center comes out clean.

5. While the omelet is baking, process the sauce ingredients in a food processor until smooth.

6. Use a spatula to loosen the edges of the omelet from the pan; slide the omelet onto a serving platter. Arrange the strawberry slices on the top of the omelet; drizzle with Nectarine Sauce. Cut into 4 wedges for serving.

PER SERVING: Cal 221/Prot 7.1g/Carb 27.9g/Fat 9g/Chol 220mg/Sod 171mg

Variations

•   If you do not have an oven-proof skillet, cook the omelet in a nonstick skillet. Use 2 large spatulas to flip the omelet to brown the second side.

•   For strawberry sauce: Substitute 1 cup sliced strawberries for the nectarine.

TIP

Don't wash strawberries or remove their caps until ready to use. Pick red, ripe strawberries at the market because they do not ripen after being picked. Store them in a moisture-proof container in the refrigerator for up to 3 days.

broiled
bananas
with orange-raisin sauce

Makes 4 servings

If you have never cooked bananas, you'll be pleasantly surprised by the way their natural sweetness is enhanced by baking. Serve this dish not only as dessert but also as part of your brunch menu.

Orange-Raisin Sauce

1¹/₄ cups fresh orange juice

1 tablespoon honey

1 tablespoon butter

¹/₄ cup golden or dark raisins (see Tips)

To Complete the Recipe

Nonstick cooking spray

4 bananas (at room temperature)

2 teaspoons fresh lemon juice

2 tablespoons butter, cut into chunks

1 tablespoon cold water

1 tablespoon cornstarch

Dash of nutmeg (preferably freshly grated), or to taste

GARNISH (OPTIONAL)   toasted finely chopped pecans or walnuts

1. Adjust the oven broiler rack to about 4 to 5 inches from the heating element; preheat the broiler.

2. Combine the orange juice, honey, butter, and raisins in a small nonstick saucepan; stir occasionally over medium heat.

3. Coat a 9-inch square baking dish with cooking spray.

4. Peel the bananas and cut them in half both lengthwise and crosswise. Arrange the strips, uncut-sides up, in the baking dish. Drizzle with the lemon juice and dot with butter. Broil for about 4 minutes, watching closely, until tender and lightly browned.

5. Meanwhile, stir together the cold water and the cornstarch in a measuring cup until smooth. Add to the Orange-Raisin Sauce, stirring constantly for about 3 minutes or until the sauce thickens. Stir in the nutmeg. Adjust the seasoning to taste.

6. For each serving, arrange 4 banana sections in a dessert bowl. Drizzle with the warm sauce and serve immediately.

PER SERVING: Cal 328/Prot 2.2g/Carb 49.8g/Fat 13.3g/Chol 25mg/Sod 97mg

ADVANCE PREPARATION   This sauce will keep for up to 2 days in a covered container in the refrigerator; reheat, stirring constantly, over low heat. Broil the bananas and assemble the dish just before serving.

Variation

• Serve the Orange-Raisin Sauce on poached fruit, such as pears.

> ## TIPS
>
> • Both dark and golden seedless raisins are made from Thompson seedless grapes. The dark raisins are sun-dried for several weeks. Golden raisins are treated with sulfur dioxide to prevent them from darkening, then dried with artificial heat, which produces a moister, plumper raisin.
>
> • Store all raisins at room temperature for several months or refrigerate them in a tightly sealed plastic bag for up to 1 year.

sautéed
apple slices
with apricot-orange sauce

Makes 4 servings

Make this simple and elegant dessert with its aromatic and colorful sauce in the fall when apples are at their best. Substitute pears in the winter.

Apricot-Orange Sauce

8 dried apricot halves (see Tips)

1 cup fresh orange juice

To Complete the Recipe

2 tablespoons butter

1 tablespoon honey

1 teaspoon pure vanilla extract

2 baking apples (at room temperature), peeled and cut into $1/4$-inch-thick slices (see Tips)

$1/4$ cup sliced almonds

$1/4$ teaspoon nutmeg (preferably freshly grated)

GARNISH (OPTIONAL)   toasted wheat germ

1. Cook the apricots in the orange juice in a medium saucepan over medium heat. When the juice begins to bubble, reduce the heat to low; cover and simmer for about 10 minutes or until the apricots are softened.

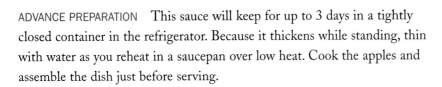

2. Meanwhile, melt the butter in a large nonstick skillet over low heat. Stir in the honey and vanilla. Add the apple and almond slices. Increase the heat to high; cook, stirring and tossing constantly, for about 5 minutes or until the apples are crisp-tender. Remove from the heat and cover to keep warm.

3. Pour the apricot-orange juice mixture into a food processor; add the nutmeg. Process until smooth.

4. To serve, arrange the warm apple slices and almonds on individual dessert plates. Top with the warm sauce and serve immediately.

PER SERVING: Cal 248/Prot 4.4g/Carb 28.3g/Fat 13g/Chol 16mg/Sod 2mg

ADVANCE PREPARATION   This sauce will keep for up to 3 days in a tightly closed container in the refrigerator. Because it thickens while standing, thin with water as you reheat in a saucepan over low heat. Cook the apples and assemble the dish just before serving.

Variations

• Substitute 4 dried peach halves for the dried apricots.

• Serve the sauce on plain yogurt, ice cream, or pancakes.

TIPS

• When chopping or dicing dried fruit, coating the blade of the knife or kitchen shears with oil will make the task easier.

• Apples suitable for cooking are Rome Beauty, Golden Delicious, Granny Smith, and Winesap. Avoid using Red Delicious and Jonathan, which are rather tender for cooking and lack the acidity that gives cooked apple dishes their characteristic flavor.

curried
fruit

Makes 6 servings

The vibrant combination of curry and ginger is compatible with a wide variety of fresh fruits; substitute or add chopped peaches, apricots, nectarines, or apples (up to 3 cups total). I especially like this served warm for dessert or brunch, but it is also delicious served chilled over vanilla ice cream.

3 tablespoons butter

$1/4$ cup light brown sugar (see Tip)

1 tablespoon curry powder

1 (11-ounce) can mandarin oranges, drained

1 pear (at room temperature), cut into 1-inch cubes

1 (8-ounce) can unsweetened pineapple chunks, drained, reserve $1/4$ cup juice

$1/2$ teaspoon minced fresh ginger

2 cups nonfat vanilla yogurt

GARNISH (OPTIONAL)   toasted coarsely chopped walnuts or pecans, a mixture of ground nuts and finely grated orange rind

1. Melt the butter in a medium nonstick saucepan over medium heat. Add the brown sugar and curry powder; stir occasionally over medium heat for about 2 minutes or until the sugar is melted and the mixture is smooth.

2. Stir in the fruit, the reserved pineapple juice, and the ginger; cover and cook for about 5 minutes or until the pear is tender.

3. To serve, spoon the warm fruit over yogurt in dessert bowls.

PER SERVING: Cal 232/Prot 3.9g/Carb 36.1g/Fat 7.1g/Chol 21mg/Sod 121mg

ADVANCE PREPARATION   To serve warm, cook and serve immediately. To serve chilled, refrigerate for up to 2 days in a covered container; do not reheat.

Variations

- Substitute 2 tablespoons honey for the brown sugar.

- Add about 1/4 cup dark or golden raisins or dried cranberries with the fruit.

TIP

To keep brown sugar from becoming hard or lumpy, keep it in an airtight jar. If it becomes hard, enclose half an apple with it in the jar, seal tightly, and let stand for 1 day; moisture from the apple will uncake the sugar.

Chocolate-Dipped Pineapple with Honey-Raspberry Sauce

chocolate-dipped
pineapple
with honey-raspberry sauce

Makes 6 servings

This is a showstopper. It always gets raves because the flavors of pineapple, raspberry, and chocolate combine wonderfully and the presentation is stunning.

1 cup Honey-Raspberry Sauce (page 189)

1 large fresh pineapple, peeled and cored
   (see Tip)

6 ounces semi-sweet chocolate

GARNISH (OPTIONAL)   sprigs of fresh mint

1. Prepare the Honey-Raspberry Sauce; refrigerate to cool.

2. Line a baking sheet or shallow pan with wax paper or kitchen parchment.

3. Slice the pineapple into ¹/₂-inch-thick rings.

4. Heat water until it simmers in the bottom pan of a double boiler over high heat, then reduce the heat to medium. Put the chocolate in the top pan insert; stir constantly as it melts. Hold a pineapple ring over the chocolate and use a spoon or rubber spatula to spread half of the ring with chocolate; then place on the baking sheet. Repeat with the remaining pineapple rings.

5. Refrigerate the pineapple, uncovered, for about ¹/₂ hour or until the chocolate sets before serving.

(continues)

6. For each serving, place a pineapple ring atop a thin layer of Honey-Raspberry Sauce on a dessert plate. Serve immediately.

PER SERVING: Cal 247/Prot 2.6g/Carb 37.7g/Fat 9.5g/Chol 0mg/Sod 1mg

ADVANCE PREPARATION   The chocolate-dipped fruit can be prepared several hours in advance; cover lightly with plastic wrap and refrigerate. Assemble the dessert just before serving.

TIP

When a pineapple is ripe, the inner leaves at the crown come out easily, the skin is orange or yellow with no traces of green, and the base of the fruit should smell sweet.

Variations

- Dip other fresh fruit into the melted chocolate such as strawberries, grapes, or orange segments.

- Dip dried fruit and nuts, such as almonds, into the chocolate. Serve them as snacks or as garnishes for a fruit platter or a dessert.

glazed oranges

Makes 4 servings

Serve this juicy, light dessert after a spicy or rich entrée. Your family and guests would never guess that such a scrumptious sauce could have been so simple to prepare.

4 oranges (at room temperature)

6 ounces frozen pineapple-orange or
   pineapple juice concentrate, thawed,
   not diluted

2 tablespoons fresh lemon juice

> **TIP**
>
> To easily remove the white membrane that clings to oranges, immerse the unpeeled orange in boiling water for 5 minutes, then peel.

GARNISH (OPTIONAL)   sprigs of fresh mint

1. Zest the peel from 2 of the oranges. Put 2 teaspoons aside for step 3.

2. To prepare the glaze, stir together the remaining zest and the juice concentrate in a small saucepan over medium-high heat. When the liquid comes to a boil, reduce the heat to medium. Cook, stirring constantly, for about 5 minutes or until the concentrate reduces and darkens slightly. Remove from heat and stir in the lemon juice; set aside to cool.

3. Meanwhile, peel the oranges (see Tip). Place them on dessert plates. Pour the glaze over each orange and top with a small mound of orange zest. Provide knives and forks for easy eating.

PER SERVING: Cal 146/Prot 2.3g/Carb 33.7g/Fat .2g/Chol 0mg/Sod 2mg

ADVANCE PREPARATION   The oranges will keep for up to 2 days in a covered container in the refrigerator. Serve chilled or at room temperature.

Variation

•   Slice the oranges or cut them into wedges; this presentation eliminates the need for serving with knives.

181

ricotta-topped
pears

Makes 4 servings

Purchase the pears several days in advance so they will be ripe and juicy. Serve this delectable dessert as a suitable finale to an Italian dinner.

1 cup nonfat ricotta cheese

1 teaspoon grated orange rind

2 tablespoons fresh orange juice

1 tablespoon honey

1/4 teaspoon almond extract

2 tablespoons slivered almonds

2 tablespoons semi-sweet chocolate chips

2 tablespoons currants or chopped raisins

2 pears, peeled, cored, and halved

GARNISH (OPTIONAL)   a sprinkling of sweetened cocoa powder

1. Combine the ricotta cheese, orange rind, orange juice, honey, and almond extract in a food processor; process until light and smooth. Stir in the almonds, chocolate chips, and currants or raisins.

2. For each serving, place a pear half, cut side up, in a dessert bowl; top with about 1/4 cup of the ricotta mixture.

PER SERVING: Cal 224/Prot 8.7g/Carb 27.7g/Fat 8.7g/Chol 20mg/Sod 77mg

ADVANCE PREPARATION   The ricotta filling will keep for up to 1 day in a covered container in the refrigerator. Slice the pears and top with the filling just before serving.

Variations

- This fruity and sweet ricotta topping can be stuffed into cannoli dessert shells (pastry tubes), available at Italian delis or gourmet shops. The mixture will fill 4 shells, which can be filled up to 3 hours before serving.

- Substitute peaches for pears.

peach
melba

Makes 4 servings

This showy dessert will impress your guests and delight your family. No one needs to know how simple it is to prepare.

1 cup Honey-Raspberry Sauce (page 189)

2 peaches (at room temperature), peeled, pitted, and halved (see Tip)

2 cups vanilla ice cream

GARNISH (OPTIONAL)   toasted almond slices, sprigs of fresh mint

1. Prepare the Honey-Raspberry Sauce. If made in advance, warm it, stirring occasionally, in a small saucepan over low heat.

2. Arrange the peach halves in dessert bowls with the cut sides up. Top each with 1 scoop of ice cream. Spoon about $1/4$ cup of the warm Honey-Raspberry Sauce over each serving and serve immediately.

PER SERVING: Cal 338/Prot 3.6g/Carb 64.1g/Fat 7.5g/Chol 29mg/Sod 55mg

---

TIP

To peel a peach, immerse it in boiling water for 1 minute, then drop the peach into cold water. Remove the peel in strips with firm downward pulls.

Variation

- Substitute plain or vanilla yogurt or vanilla frozen yogurt for the ice cream.

frozen
banana-berry
parfaits

Makes 4 servings

Frozen bananas work like magic—they create a dessert with a rich-tasting, creamy texture. Plan ahead for freezing the bananas (a great use for those that are just past their prime for eating fresh) and prepare the dessert in minutes just before serving.

3 frozen bananas, peeled

$1/2$ cup nonfat plain yogurt

2 tablespoons honey

1 cup sliced strawberries

1 cup blueberries (see Tip)

TIP

Select blueberries that are uniform in shape and deep blue in color. They should have a powdery look, called "bloom," which is a sign of freshness. Blueberries will keep for about 1 week in the refrigerator; wash just before using.

GARNISH (OPTIONAL)   grating of semi-sweet chocolate, whole strawberries

1. Just before serving, cut the bananas into 1-inch-thick slices while still frozen. Combine the yogurt and honey in a food processor. Gradually add the banana slices and process until smooth and creamy.

2. Spoon the banana mixture into parfait glasses, alternating with layers of strawberries and blueberries. Serve immediately.

PER SERVING: Cal 173/Prot 2.9g/Carb 39g/Fat .6g/Chol 1mg/Sod 23mg

ADVANCE PREPARATION   In advance, peel the bananas, wrap them in a plastic bag, and freeze overnight or for up to 2 weeks. When making the dessert, prepare only the amount you need for serving; refreezing is unsatisfactory.

fruit
smoothie

Makes 4 servings

I always keep some frozen fruit on hand for making this recipe. It's a satisfying summer cooler and an ideal use for fruit on the verge of overripening, or you can use packaged frozen mixed fruit from the supermarket. Make this for a spur-of-the-moment dessert that will please both kids and adults alike.

3 cups frozen mixed chopped fruit (cantaloupe, bananas, strawberries, peaches, or others of your choice); do not thaw

1 cup apple juice

GARNISH (OPTIONAL)   kiwi slices (see Tip), strawberries, raspberries

Blend the fruit and juice in a food processor or blender until smooth, occasionally pushing down fruit chunks for uniform consistency. Serve immediately; the mixture melts quickly.

PER SERVING: Cal 65/Prot .8g/Carb 15.4g/Fat 0g/Chol 0mg/Sod 1mg

ADVANCE PREPARATION   In advance, peel the fruit (if necessary), wrap in a plastic bag, and freeze overnight or for up to 2 weeks. Fruit Smoothies are best if served immediately after preparing. If necessary, the mixture can be frozen for up to 30 minutes before serving; if frozen longer, the mixture becomes icy.

Variations

- Use one type of frozen fruit rather than a mixture of fruits; strawberries are especially good.

- Substitute fresh orange juice for the apple juice.

pear
sorbet

Makes 4 servings

Use this simple technique to make other sorbet flavors, such as mandarin orange or peach.

1 (16-ounce) can unsweetened sliced
    pears, drained and frozen

1/4 cup fresh orange juice

1 tablespoon honey

GARNISH (OPTIONAL)   toasted sliced almonds, strawberries

1. In advance, drain the pears and freeze in a freezer container at least overnight.

2. Ten minutes before serving, remove the container from the freezer and let stand at room temperature so the pears will soften slightly.

3. Just before serving, process the pears, orange juice, and honey in a food processor until smooth. Serve immediately.

PER SERVING: Cal 100/Prot .1g/Carb 25g/Fat 0g/Chol 0mg/Sod 9mg

ADVANCE PREPARATION   Freeze the pears at least overnight or for up to 2 weeks. Serve the dessert immediately after preparing.

maple
hot chocolate
sauce

Makes 1 cup

The flavors of chocolate and maple blend artfully to create a rich sauce to serve for special occasions. Use it to top the Vanilla Poached Pears (page 166), ice cream, or frozen yogurt.

4 ounces unsweetened chocolate

2 tablespoons butter

3/4 cup pure maple syrup (see Tips)

1/4 cup skim milk

1. Heat water until it simmers in the bottom pan of a double boiler over high heat (see Tips), then reduce the heat to medium. Put the chocolate in the top pan insert; stir constantly as it melts. Add the butter and continue stirring as it melts. Add the maple syrup and milk, stirring constantly as the sauce heats.

2. Pour the sauce into a food processor or blender; process until very smooth and creamy. Serve warm.

PER TABLESPOON: Cal 65/Prot .4g/Carb 7.6g/Fat 3.7g/Chol 4mg/Sod 19mg

ADVANCE PREPARATION   This sauce will keep for up to 1 week in a tightly closed container in the refrigerator. When chilled, it becomes very thick; thin with milk when reheating. To prevent burning, stir as you reheat the sauce in the top pan insert of a double boiler.

TIPS

- For the best flavor, buy pure maple syrup, not "maple-flavored" syrup, which is stretched with corn syrup. Once opened, maple syrup should be refrigerated. If crystals develop, place the container in a pan of hot water until they disappear.

- The water level in the bottom pan of a double boiler should not touch the top pan insert.

honey-raspberry
sauce

Makes 1 cup

Without a doubt, this is my number one fruit sauce, not only for some of the dessert recipes in this book but also for chopped fresh or poached fruit, ice cream, pancakes, and waffles. Best of all is my occasional decadence: a layer of this sauce spread on a dessert plate, topped with a slice of my favorite flourless chocolate cake from the Italian bakery.

1 (10-ounce) package frozen slightly
    sweetened ("lite") raspberries (2 cups)

2 tablespoons honey

$^1/_4$ cup water

1 tablespoon cornstarch (see Tip)

1. Combine the raspberries and honey in a small nonstick saucepan. Stir constantly over low heat, until just below boiling. Remove from heat.

2. Stir together the water and cornstarch in a measuring cup until smooth. Add to the honey–berry mixture; stir constantly for about 5 minutes or until the sauce is thickened and smooth.

3. Strain the sauce through a coarse sieve atop a mixing bowl; as it drains, stir occasionally with a wooden spoon. Discard the seeds.

> **TIP**
>
> Cornstarch and arrowroot give a clear quality to a soup or sauce, while flour makes it opaque. Use slightly less arrowroot than cornstarch (about $2^1/_2$ teaspoons arrowroot to 1 tablespoon cornstarch) if you are making a substitution.

PER TABLESPOON: Cal 44/Prot .2g/Carb 10.8g/Fat 0g/Chol 0mg/Sod 1mg

ADVANCE PREPARATION   The sauce will keep for up to 5 days in a tightly closed container in the refrigerator. Because it thickens while standing, thin with water when reheating.

Variations

- For strawberry sauce: Substitute frozen strawberries for the raspberries; no need to strain.

- Substitute lime juice for the water and increase the honey to 3 tablespoons—delicious served on fresh papaya slices.

chapter 7

The Vegetarian Entertainer

IT MAY SEEM CHALLENGING TO SERVE A VEGETARIAN

meal for guests, especially those who eat meat. Remind

yourself that everyone likes good food, so if you serve

truly tasty dishes, you're sure to get a favorable reaction.

When you plan the menu, remember that long hours in

the kitchen aren't necessary to produce a dinner party

that comes off perfectly, but it does take careful thought

and some advance planning. See the following pages for

some tips to keep in mind.

Tips for the Vegetarian Entertainer

- Keep the menu simple, especially when cooking for more than six. An entrée that includes a protein source, vegetables, and a starch can stand alone on the dinner plate with a simple salad accompaniment.

- For small groups, serve in courses. For large groups, consider serving buffet-style.

- Never select more than one recipe requiring last-minute attention.

- Some dishes can be partially made ahead. For example, toss a pasta sauce made in advance with hot, freshly cooked pasta.

- If some of your favorite party recipes are time-consuming, consider using one or more of these 15-minute recipes as accompaniments.

- Most of my recipes were developed to serve from four to six, but many can be easily expanded to serve large groups. Allow extra time for preparation; it usually takes longer to chop more ingredients and a larger volume may require a longer cooking time. Also, when expanding recipes, you rarely need to increase the herbs and other seasonings in the same proportion as the major ingredients. Rule of thumb: When doubling a recipe, add $1^1/_2$ times the amount of herbs. Then add more to taste.

- If you are preparing foods in advance, always cover and refrigerate them, then reheat just before serving. Some dishes, such as dips, need only to be brought to room temperature. Some of the more pungent seasonings such as curry powder and red pepper flakes intensify in flavor as they stand.

- Arrange your ingredients, cooking equipment, and serving dishes so they are convenient for last-minute preparations.

- Set the scene; use creative table settings but don't overdo. Elegant simplicity is always pleasing.

- Add colorful, and sometimes surprising, garnishes. Even if the meal was prepared quickly, these extra touches will show that the food was prepared with care.

chapter 8

How to Plan a Vegetarian Meal

MENU PLANNING IS THE MOST IMPORTANT ASPECT OF

serving a really superb meal. You may want to begin by

selecting the entrée, then choose accompaniments that

will complement it. Other times a fine meatless meal can

be composed of two or three complementary courses of

equal importance. Sometimes, an event can be planned

around another course, such as a special dessert, pre-

ceded by a simple, light entrée.

Tips for Planning a Vegetarian Meal

Use these guidelines for balancing elements when you are planning a complete vegetarian menu:

- *Nutrition*: Include a protein source. Remember that it can be in any of the courses, including dessert. This can be as simple as serving tofu, eggs, or cheese; also consult the list of complementary food combinations on page xv.

- *Variety*: Don't repeat predominant ingredients or distinct flavorings in more than one course.

- *Flavors*: Contrast potent flavors with milder ones and sweetness with tartness.

- *Color*: Use a variety of colors, and add vivid garnishes to less colorful dishes.

- *Texture*: Balance creamy, smooth textures with crispness; raw foods with cooked foods.

- *Substance*: Balance a rich and filling dish with something light.

- *Seasonal elements*: Serve warming foods in cold weather, and lighter foods when the temperature rises.

- *Flamboyance*: Plan for one dish to be the star of the menu, the others supporting players.

- *Surprises*: Add the unexpected. Be innovative. Use edible flowers for garnishing; or if the quality is good, use out-of-season fruit, like strawberries in December.

- *Theme*: Carry out a theme in your menu. The inspiration can be a certain cuisine or a seasonal celebration.

- *Dietary restrictions and food preferences*: Please your family and guests with what suits them best. Add or substitute ingredients. You can please the meat-eaters in your family by adding meat or serving meat with many of these recipes.

The following menus, featuring recipes in this book, have earned me compliments from my family and friends. I suggest also recording some of your personal favorites.

Southeast Asian Dinner

- Baba Ghannouj with Pita Crisps (pages 29 and 63)
- Thai Cucumber Salad (page 86)
- Vegetable Curry with brown rice (page 138)
- Mixed Fruit Chutney (page 15)
- Broiled Bananas with Orange-Raisin Sauce (page 172)

Fall Luncheon

- Puréed Vegetable Soup with Broccoli Florets (page 48)
- Almond Butter-Wheat Germ Sticks (page 61)
- Sautéed Apple Slices with Apricot-Orange Sauce (page 174)

Cool Summer Supper

- Chunky Garden Gazpacho (page 56)
- Pita Crisps (page 63)
- Couscous-Currant Salad with Lemon Dressing (page 96)
- Frozen Banana-Berry Parfaits (page 185)

Light and Fresh Feast

- Asian Stew (page 42)
- Pasta with Chinese Tahini Sauce (page 124)
- Pear Sorbet (page 187)

Simple Soup Dinner

- Almond-Mushroom Pâté with crusty bread (page 28)

- Quick Pea Soup (page 46)

- Tossed green salad with cherry tomatoes, cheese cubes, and Honey-Poppyseed Dressing (page 69)

- Glazed Oranges (page 181)

Family Dinner

- Savory Nut Burgers with Zesty Tomato Sauce (page 150)

- Steamed asparagus spears (page xxx)

- Rice and Spinach Salad with Asian Vinaigrette (page 83)

- Baked Peaches with Chutney Stuffing (page 169)

Festive Omelet Dinner

- Guacamole Omelet with Tomato Hot Sauce (page 156)

- Basil-Bean Salad (page 101)

- Fruit Smoothie (page 186)

Menu Italiano

- Pasta Marinara on Beds of Spinach (page 113)

- Tossed green salad with Summer Peach Vinaigrette (page 74)

- Vanilla Poached Pears with Maple Hot Chocolate Sauce (page 166)

Do-Ahead Party Buffet

- Pasta Salad Primavera with Herbed Tomato Sauce (page 99)

- French bread with Pesto Herb Spread (page 17)

- Ricotta-Topped Pears (page 182)

Morning Glory Brunch

- Italian Garden Frittata with Marinara Sauce (page 160)

- Assorted breads and muffins

- Curried Fruit (page 176)

Stir-Fry Special

- Spinach and Strawberry Salad with Pepper Vinaigrette (page 79)

- Vegetable Stir-Fry with Ginger Sauce on brown rice (page 140)

- Chocolate-Dipped Pineapple with Honey-Raspberry Sauce (page 179)

Pasta Picnic

- Pasta Shells with Lemon Vinaigrette (page 114)

- French bread with Pesto Herb Spread (page 17)

- Maple Oranges Amandine (page 165)

index

Page numbers in *italics* refer to illustrations.